PACKER PRIDE

FOR THE LOVE OF LAMBEAU, LOMBARDI & CHEESEHEADS

ALAN ROSS

Cumberland House
Nashville, Tennessee

PACKER PRIDE
PUBLISHED BY CUMBERLAND HOUSE PUBLISHING, INC.
431 Harding Industrial Drive
Nashville, Tennessee 37211-3160

Cover design: Gore Studio, Inc., Nashville, Tennessee
Text design: John Mitchell

Library of Congress Cataloging-in-Publication Data

Ross, Alan, 1944–
   Packer pride : for the love of Lambeau, Lombardi & cheeseheads / Alan Ross
     p.   cm.
   Includes bibliographical references and index.
   ISBN 1-58182-417-3 (pbk. : alk. paper)
   1. Green Bay Packers (Football team)—History. 2. Green Bay Packers
(Football team)—Miscellanea. I. Title.
GV956.G7R64 2004
796.332'64'0977561—dc22   2004009336

Printed in Canada

3 4 5 6 7—10 09 08 07 06

For Don Wojcik,
a Windy City follower of the Pack,
and as always, to Karol, my constant strength,
support, and committed love.

A most special thanks to Sheila Randolph,
my own personal interlibrary loner
and self-sacrificing friend.

Vince Lombardi, legendary Packer head coach

CONTENTS

Introduction   7
Remembrance   9

1   Packer Tradition   13
2   Packer Pride   23
3   The Green and Gold   29
4   Packer Character   45
5   Packer Humor   67
6   The School of Lombardi   79
7   Packer Legends   99
8   Shrine to No. 14   135
9   Tales from the Tundra   145
10 Famous Moments   159
11 The All-Time Green Bay Packers Team   191
12 Fields of Play   215
13 Rivalries   227
14 The Locker Room   241
15 Packers World Championship Rosters   249

Bibliography   263
Index   267

INTRODUCTION

For many, the love of the Green Bay Packers lies in the warm thought that a cherished link to the era of embryonic pro football, born in the small towns of America, still exists—one of the few 19th-century "town teams" to make it in professional football. In this day of climate-controlled indoor stadiums, artificial turf (thankfully on the wane), and mega-million dollar player contracts, it's not only comforting but vitally essential that the Packers are alive and well—the solitary reminder of the sport's by-gone days; the smallest city to have an NFL team; the town team that successfully fights toe-to-toe with large market foes.

Every team has its rabid following. But Green Bay is a little something else. Besides being the only nonprofit team in football, the Packers boast 111,507 stockholders from around the world, who own more than 4.7 million shares and represent the only publicly operated major sports team in the United States. Green Bay Packers, Inc. also includes a 45-member board elected by those stockholders. In short, it's the people's team; or as Brett Favre likes to say about his Packers: the true America's team.

Green Bay is one of only two current NFL franchises (Arizona is the other) that can trot out a team history dating back to the pre-NFL days. The Packers' illustrious vault of icons begins with Curly Lambeau, the player, later the legendary coach, and runs through the brilliant Vince Lombardi dynasty, before surging into the 21st century behind stars like Favre. Topping it all is the venerable reverence reserved for the game's most sacred ground—Lambeau Field.

Inside these pages, you'll travel through Packerland, as experienced by the players, coaches, opponents, and members of the media.

For Cheeseheads everywhere, it's pure cheddar.

REMEMBRANCE

The bitter New York City wind whipped like a vengeful assassin. It was 7 a.m., Monday, December 17, 1962. Temperature 21 degrees.

A serpentine line wrapped itself one and a half times around the massive circumference of Yankee Stadium, home to not only baseball's diamond gods, the New York Yankees, but also, at one time, to the NFL's New York Giants. And I, fool, was in it.

Ten thousand tickets were being made available to the proletariat (read: non-season ticket holders) for the NFL Championship Game encounter between the Giants and the Green Bay Packers two weeks hence, on December 30. For the second and last time ever, the Stadium would host an NFL title game.

I was a college freshman then. The previous night, Fordham University's Welsh Chorale had staged a concert and a party was held afterward. Upperclassmen in the chorale chided us yearlings to keep pace with them, veteran drinkers that they were. Heavy imbibing took place, upholding that most time-honored of collegiate traditions. Earlier that same day, I had told friends of my early Monday morning plan: to be at Yankee Stadium at least two hours before the ticket booths opened and snatch up a treasured game ticket to the one-game World Series of pro football.

It was with the worst of hangovers that I arrived at the Stadium, concluding two hours of sleep from the prior evening's bacchanal. To my inexpressible chagrin, the lengthy line took on the appearance of one of those endless, forlorn welfare lines of the Great Depression. Obviously, thousands of others had the same plan as mine. Some fanatics even arrived at midnight to stake their place. The Oklahoma Land Rush couldn't have been any worse. My guts heaved and my head howled. Where could I just lie down and die! But like slow-moving traffic crawling along the Hutchison River Parkway at rush hour, the stoic line of Giants faithful relentlessly inched its way round and round toward the target destination—those pearly gated ticket windows. No rest awaited the weary; no bathroom break, no breakfast snack. In my depleted state, every minute felt like a week, the pain in my belly from the gross over-indulgence of sherry bending me over like a limp noodle.

An agonizing five and a half hours later, my tank on empty, my frozen ears having fallen off three hours earlier, and with nothing but the manic-driven goal of a championship game ticket keeping me semi-upright, we finally came within 20 yards of the ticket booths. A surge of adrenaline created a brief wisp of second wind. It was 12:30 p.m. Then suddenly, preposterously, a mournful wail collectively groaned by the throng ahead coursed past us with a nauseating wave.

The ticket windows slammed in unison. SOLD OUT!

Thirteen days later, while Jim Taylor demoralized the great Giants defense in one of pro football's most stirring illustrations of true grit, and while Jerry Kramer kicked three field goals as 40-mile-an-hour wind gusts blasted the brick-hard Stadium floor, I listened to the Packers' 16–7 triumph—on radio. The loathsome "blackout" rule for television was in effect for the New York area.

That's as close as I ever got to seeing an NFL Championship Game.

And I've never waited in line for anything in my life since.

— A.R.

PACKER
TRADITION

It's the biggest little major league city in the world.

Anonymous former
Packer player
on Green Bay, Wisconsin

Anyone who knows football history realizes what the Green Bay Packers mean to our game. This is hallowed ground.

Ron Wolf
Packers general manager
(1992–2001)

Curly Lambeau brought the forward pass to Green Bay after playing one season under Rockne [at Notre Dame] in 1918 and pioneered its use in professional football.

John B. Torinus
author

Although Green Bay fielded town teams as early as 1896, the generally accepted date for the Green Bay Packers birth is August 14, 1919.

Don Davenport
author

The nickname "Packers" evolved from the 1919 city team that was sponsored by the Indian Packing Company.

Don Davenport

When I came to Green Bay, I embraced the tradition. They had this rich, rich history. That intrigued me. I figured that's what I'm here for, to be a part of Packers history. That means everything to me.

Brett Favre
quarterback (1992–)

The history of Curly Lambeau and Green Bay football was as glorious as it was tenuous. His first team [in 1919], which played against clubs in Wisconsin and Michigan's Upper Peninsula, was a powerhouse, winning 10 straight and outscoring the opposition 565 points to 12. . . . Matters on the financial side were less splendid. The team did not charge for admission, collecting donations by passing the hat.

David Maraniss
author

Profits were allowed to pile up and were divided among the team members at the close of the season. Each player drew $16 from the kitty, an average of about $1.45 per man per game.

Red Grange
storied Chicago Bears
Hall of Fame halfback
(1925, 1929–34),
on the 1919 Packers

The Packers fielded their first professional team in 1921, with a roster made up of players nicknamed Cub, Tubby, Curly, Toody, Jab, and Cowboy.

Don Davenport

When the Packers played the Stapletons over on Staten Island in metropolitan New York, they dressed in their hotel rooms in downtown New York, took a bus to the Staten Island ferry, then rode the boat over to the island, where they proceeded on foot to the stadium.

John B. Torinus

Thompson Stadium, the Stapletons' home field, had no dressing quarters. Green Bay won that game, 21–3, on Nov. 27, 1932, before 3,500, the smallest crowd to see a Packers game home or away all season.

Mike Michalske recalled once that when they played in Pottsville, Pennsylvania, the team dressed in the fire station two blocks away from the stadium, then ran down to the field for the game and dragged their butts back afterwards.

Larry Names
author

In the 1940s, the Lumberjack Band transformed mere accomplished musicians into a complete marching band, performing shows before the game and again at halftime.

Daniel Edelstein
author

The idea of Green Bay as "Titletown, USA" meant something to old-time fans but not to the kids. The last time the Packers won a championship Lyndon Johnson was president.

Brett Favre
before guiding Green Bay
to victory in Super Bowl XXXI

For us to be validated as a great team, we've first got to prove our greatness to the Willie Woods, the Willie Davises, the Bart Starrs, all those great old players. I'm convinced that the Ray Nitschkes and those guys probably don't think we could have played with them.

Sean Jones
defensive end (1994–96)

Lombardi had used the sweep in New York and had originally borrowed it from the playbook of the Los Angeles Rams, but once he arrived in Green Bay he transformed it into something that was singularly identified with him and his Packers.

David Maraniss

Thurston and Kramer became the symbols of the Packer sweep, patrolling the turf ahead of Hornung, circling deep and around the corner, forearms out, ready to strike, Nos. 63 and 64 in green and gold.

David Maraniss

There couldn't have been a Lombardi if there hadn't been a Lambeau, at least not in Green Bay.

Lee Remmel
*Packers executive director
of public relations*

Lambeau might have cast the only shadow in sports under which Lombardi felt any noticeable shade.

Steve Cameron
author

The Lambeau Leap, man, that's a big deal for us now. People love it and so do the players. Robert Brooks is the best at the leap. He jumps right into the fans' laps. He's got springs. . . . Damn he's good. He once told me that he felt like a rock star jumping off a stage and into the arms of his fans.

Brett Favre
on a modern Green Bay tradition, the post-touchdown catapult into the stands

It's the best feeling in the world, and I don't think you could do it anywhere but here.

Robert Brooks
wide receiver (1992–98),
"Father" of the Lambeau Leap

Mike Holmgren embraced the tradition of the Packers. He brought in all the old players from those Lombardi teams and held their success up as an example.

Brett Favre
on the former Packers head coach

I want my team to be remembered like the old Packers. Fuzzy, Bart, and Ray. Jim Taylor and Paul Hornung. Vince Lombardi. How many other Super Bowl teams are there that you can name so many guys off of?

Brett Favre

PACKER PRIDE

I know the whole town is behind us in spirit. . . . We've shown the other clubs that we are not a weak sister. Let's show them that we don't talk this game here, but come out to see it, too!

> Earl L. (Curly) Lambeau
> *Packers co-founder, player, and*
> *31-year head coach (1919–49)*

In the old days, [Curly] Lambeau had survived by his wits, once persuading a fan to auction his roadster to keep the team out of hock.

David Maraniss

The team has been in Green Bay since 1919. Kids go to Lombardi Middle School. People drive down Lombardi Avenue. The stadium is named after Curly Lambeau. Check out the yellow pages. There are 40 businesses in town that use the Packers' name.

Brett Favre

I try to play so I can live with myself.

Willie Davis
Hall of Fame defensive end
(1960–69)

Last year an after-dinner speaker referred to me as the Vagabond Halfback, and because of my philosophy, taken from the French, which is to be as amusing and spectacular as possible, I did not object to being called a vagabond. Of late, however, I notice Chicago is making public enemies of vagrants, and I wish at this time to drop the appendage. The Israelites, if I know my Bible, were in bondage for 40 years. I have not been in bondage, but I have been in vagabondage for quite a while, and I'm all through. Last year, when the Packers won the championship, I said I was in the greatest town in the world, and I'm still glad to be in it—Green Bay, the home of the perpetual fatted calf.

> **Johnny "Blood" McNally**
> *Hall of Fame halfback*
> *(1929–33, 1935–36),*
> *speaking at the celebration of*
> *the Packers' 1930 NFL*
> *championship, Beaumont Hotel*
> *dining room, Green Bay*

It was about three in the morning. I was wearing a Green Bay fireman's helmet and throwing colored beads to Packers fans down on Bourbon Street. There must've been a thousand fans standing down there, and I was leading them in chants of "Go Pack Go" and "We're No. 1."

Brett Favre
after the Packers' victory
in Super Bowl XXXI

People will come up to me, grown men, and tell me stories of following the Packers when they were three years old. Or about their daddy willing them season tickets when he passed away. Some will have tears in their eyes when they talk about the team.

Brett Favre

Before the [1996] divisional playoff game against San Francisco, Green Bay got hit with a foot of snow. Lambeau Field was buried. . . . Ted Eisenreich, the Packers' building supervisor, let everyone know that he needed 200 people to dig out the field. The Packers paid six dollars an hour. So many people showed up that dozens had to be turned away. Some people even said that they'd work for free. Amazing.

Brett Favre

When Lombardi said, "You were chosen to be a Packer," he made it sound like something unique and wonderful.

Willie Davis

When Reggie White's Inner City Church [in Knoxville, Tennessee] burned down, people in the area raised and then donated more than a quarter of a million dollars to rebuild it. That's Green Bay for you.

Brett Favre

That made me so proud to be a Packer.

Ray Nitschke
Nov. 5, 1972, on the tremendous ovation he received upon entering the game, one of his last, as a substitute in Green Bay's 34–24 victory over San Francisco

He [Vince Lombardi] built up the 1961 NFL Championship Game [vs. New York] so the thing was, you were defending the pride of Green Bay as much as you were the pride of the Packers.

Willie Davis

THE GREEN AND GOLD

The first player of national reputation to join the Packers was Howard "Cub" Buck from the University of Wisconsin, a giant of a center who anchored the Packer line from 1921 through 1925. The next year saw Jug Earp arriving to take over the center spot as Buck moved to tackle.

John B. Torinus

The first real superstar hired by the Packers was Verne Lewellen of Nebraska, a big-back halfback and super punter who came in 1924.

John B. Torinus

Santana Dotson's quickness and Gilbert Brown's size make a terrific twosome. Gilbert's big enough to call it a threesome.

Brett Favre
on Green Bay's defensive tackle pair of the mid 1990s

Lewellen was one of the few men of his day who could do it all: run, pass, catch, kick, block, and tackle. He was the complete football player.

Larry Names
on halfback Verne Lewellen
(1924–32)

Lambeau brought in a series of colorful stars over the ensuing years, the rambunctious halfback John McNally, known as Johnny Blood, the quarterbacks Cecil Isbell and Arnie Herber, the fullback Clarke Hinkle, and the greatest receiver of his era in professional football, Don Hutson of Alabama.

David Maraniss

Three of the greatest pass catchers in the history of the NFL have worn Packer uniforms: Don Hutson, James Lofton, and Sterling Sharpe. . . . And let us not forget Boyd Dowler, Billy Howton, and Max McGee. None of them ever embarrassed Green Bay on the field. Although Johnny Blood doesn't have the numbers, his contemporaries called him the greatest receiver of his time.

Larry Names

Lavvie Dilweg was an All-American end at Marquette before joining the Packers in 1927. He made All-Pro in 1931 then practiced law in Green Bay after retiring from football. He was later elected to Congress from Wisconsin's Eighth District.

John B. Torinus

I have always rated Dilweg as the greatest end who ever brought me down.

Red Grange

Even his greatest rivals will admit that Red Dunn was a quarterback who sacrificed every personal ambition to give the Packers victory. He was the ideal field general in the years from 1927 to 1931, scoring only a single touchdown, while contributing 46 points after touchdowns and two field goals.

> **Arch Ward**
> *illustrious longtime* Chicago Tribune *sports editor (1930–55)/author/promoter*

As a field general, Dunn was superior to any man who wore a Packer uniform to that time.

> **Larry Names**
> *on quarterback Red Dunn (1927–31)*

I rate Hubbard, tackle; Michalske, guard; Earp, center; and Dilweg, end, as the best men in their positions I ever encountered in competition.

Red Grange

Halfbacks and fullbacks did the passing in Curly Lambeau's offenses. Arnie Herber and Cecil Isbell weren't quarterbacks, they were halfbacks who passed the ball as well as ran with it.

Larry Names

Tobin Rote, a big rugged running back with a strong arm, was stationed in Coach Gene Ronzani's innovative shotgun formation 10 yards back from the center. He would either pass or run for his life. . . . Rote proved what he could do with a good line in front of him and capable receivers when he went to the Detroit Lions and took them to the 1957 NFL championship.

John B. Torinus
on the early-1950s Packers
quarterback (1950–56)

The Packers didn't have a true quarterback in the modern sense [T-formation] . . . until the 1950s. . . . Bob Thomason was probably the first modern quarterback to play for the Packers.

Larry Names

One of the best defenders I played against was Green Bay's Bobby Dillon. He had one eye! I could never figure out which one he was blind in. I never had any great games against the Packers because of him. He was an excellent pass defense man. He was one of the best the Packers ever had.

> **Harlon Hill**
> *three-time Pro Bowl end,*
> *Chicago Bears (1954–61)*

Stellar defender Bobby Dillon was All-Pro seven out of his eight NFL seasons and played in four Pro Bowls. What made his performance so impressive was that he had sight in only one eye.

> **John B. Torinus**
> *on the brilliant Packers safety*
> *(1952–59)*

He told me he believed I was the finest defensive back he had ever seen.

Bobby Dillon
on Packers head coach Gene Ronzani's appraisal of his star safety, after Dillon's four-interception game against the Detroit Lions, Thanksgiving Day 1953—a Packers record that still stands

It appears only two things have kept Dillon out of the Hall of Fame: He didn't play long enough and didn't play for a winner.

Jerry Poling
author

He's a good short-trap blocker, and he's got enough quickness, size, strength, and determination so that, when he and Jerry [Kramer] come swinging around that corner together like a pair of matched Percherons, you can see that defensive man's eyeballs pop.

Vince Lombardi
on Fuzzy Thurston

Somewhere along the line, the people in Canton should recognize Dave Robinson for what he was. There was no linebacker in football at the time more domineering than Dave. He was smart, bigger than most of them. He would just flat-out punish you.

Willie Davis

VERNON J. BIEVER

Jerry Kramer

Jerry Kramer has the perfect devil-may-care attitude it takes to play this game. He not only ignores the small hurts but the large ones, too. The evidence of his indifference is all over his body.

> **Vince Lombardi**
> *head coach (1959–67)*

Paul and Bart and Jimmy are in the Hall of Fame. Somebody must have blocked for them.

> **Fuzzy Thurston**
> *guard (1959–67),*
> *on teammate Jerry Kramer's*
> *failure to get the necessary votes*
> *for induction into the Pro*
> *Football Hall of Fame,*
> *in January 1997*

Em says the most intelligent things before the games. He sizes up the situation perfectly.

> **Bart Starr**
> *quarterback (1956–71),*
> *on Hall of Fame defensive back*
> *Emlen Tunnell (1959–61),*
> *whom Lombardi brought to*
> *Green Bay after 11 seasons with*
> *the New York Giants*

Mike's coached the best. Montana. Young. BYU. Super Bowls. MVPs. I knew he'd been around great players, great organizations. I knew he knew what he was talking about.

> **Brett Favre**
> *on former head coach*
> *Mike Holmgren*

He is one tough s.o.b. and a great guy to have on your side, whether you're in a game or a fight or both. I think he'd give himself up for me. I'd do the same for him. . . . . Frankie is like having a 300-pound Mafia hit man on your side.

Brett Favre
on center Frank Winters
(1992–2002)

Whenever someone asks about Edgar Bennett, I tell them he's the best all-purpose back in the league. . . . I tell him he's the best bad-weather back I've ever seen. He'll get mad and say, "What about the good days?"

Brett Favre

Antonio Freeman . . . has all the tools. He's strong. He's fast. He's smart. He's also one of the best double-move guys in the league. Antonio really sells it.

> **Brett Favre**
> *on the Packers' wide receiver*

Robert Brooks is the hardest-working man in football. He's a lot like Jerry Rice. Super guy. Helluva receiver. Hard worker.

> **Brett Favre**
> *on the former Green Bay wideout*

He's as good at what he does as anyone in the league.

> **Ron Wolf**
> *on punt/kickoff return ace*
> *Desmond Howard*

PACKER
CHARACTER

The thing that develops character in people is adverse situations; the discipline and conditioning programs they went through, the punishment and suffering, they all tend to develop character. And once you develop character, then you develop hope in all situations. . . . Vince [Lombardi] developed a lot of character in his players, character that a lot of them probably never would have had without the leadership and discipline he developed in them.

Tom Landry
Dallas Cowboys Hall of Fame head coach

The game of pro football as we know it today was created by dreamers like Curly Lambeau and George Calhoun, who never took the time to question whether a little town like Green Bay could compete in a national football league. Remember this: They had no revenue even from radio in those early days. . . . They lived on gate receipts and on their wits and their hype. Theirs was a constant battle to sell people on a game most of them had never seen before.

John B. Torinus

Once you have agreed upon the price you and your family must pay for success, it enables you to forget the price.

Vince Lombardi

Success demands singleness of purpose.

Vince Lombardi

Let's make 'em like it!

Johnny "Blood" McNally

exhorting his teammates during a 20–6 win over the New York Giants at the Polo Grounds, Nov. 29, 1929, in which Blood pounced on a Giants fumble and scored the Packers' last touchdown, keeping Green Bay undefeated at 10–0 atop the league

Any criticism I make of anyone, I make only because he's a ballplayer not playing up to his potential. Any fine I levy on anyone, I levy because he's hurting not only himself but 35 other men.

Vince Lombardi

I didn't party in high school. I was at home on Friday nights doing push-ups and sit-ups. My dad didn't make me do that, but somewhere along the way, I developed a strong commitment to that type of discipline by just being around him, by talking with him, and by watching him coach.

Brett Favre

Irvin Favre coached all three of his sons—Scott, Brett, and Jeff—at Hancock North Central High School in Hancock County, Miss.

His teammates and friends, simply put, would take a bullet for him. Probably because they trust he would do the same for them.

Chris Havel
author,
on Brett Favre

When you've been cut four times and have a wife and two kids, you've just got to make it. You don't only owe it to your family, you owe it to your life.

Fuzzy Thurston

In this game, you can't think you saw something. You've *got* to see it.

Mike Holmgren
head coach (1992–1998)

Mike's capacity for patience was huge. Harping on me was just his way of getting me to where I am today. It's not an easy thing to admit, but as tough as he was on me, I'll be forever grateful.

Brett Favre
on Mike Holmgren

Of all the games I've done, that final drive was the greatest triumph of will over adversity I'd ever seen. It was a thing of beauty.

> Ray Scott
>
> *longtime Packers play-by-play announcer, on the legendary conclusion of the Ice Bowl, Dec. 31, 1967, when Packers quarterback Bart Starr drove Green Bay 68 yards on a frozen field for the winning touchdown, taking the final yard himself with 16 seconds left*

Some of us will do our jobs well and some will not, but we will all be judged by only one thing—the result.

> Vince Lombardi

We owe those guys. Those guys beat us at home last time, so it's a payback. It's called a rematch. It's just like playing a Madden video game; you get beat and you want a rematch.

> **Donald Driver**
> *wide receiver (1999–), after the Packers defeated the Seattle Seahawks, 33–27, in overtime in a 2003 NFC Wild Card game, to advance to the Divisional Playoffs against the Philadelphia Eagles, a team that had beaten Green Bay, 17–14, at Lambeau Field in November on a last-minute touchdown pass*

Quarterback Lynn Dickey dealt with pain nearly every day of his career. I have never seen anybody quite like him. We put him through a torturous rehabilitation program that had no precedent. Lynn didn't even have enough strength to lift light weights. The feeling around the locker room was that he would never take another snap. But knowing Lynn, I don't think he ever seriously thought about quitting. And sure enough, he had several productive seasons with the Packers after that. Most people wouldn't go to a tea party with some of the injuries he had.

Domenic Gentile
Packers trainer (1961–92),
on quarterback Lynn Dickey
(1976–77, 1979–85)

There are going to be times when you're hurting, but the same thing is true in life. Sometimes you get hit hard, and sometimes you don't feel like getting back up. But I always have, on and off the field.

Brett Favre

Sterling Sharpe played most of the 1990 season with three fractured ribs. Most fans would never go to work on Monday with three fractured ribs. That season, Sharpe caught 67 passes for 1,105 yards and six touchdowns.

Domenic Gentile

Bart Starr didn't wear a rib protector until late in his career. There was nothing on the market at that time, so we devised a flak jacket for him to wear. It was made of hard plastic and is now displayed in the Packer Hall of Fame. The jacket weighed only about eight or nine ounces, but Bart thought it was too heavy, so we eventually came up with a cloth vest lined with plastic inserts. It looked like a bandolier.

Domenic Gentile

Having the respect of the fans and my teammates is more important to me than doubling my salary.

Brett Favre

I have a little bit of a knot in there or something.

Bob Brown
defensive tackle (1966–73),
to trainer Domenic Gentile dur-
ing the course of a game against
Minnesota. Brown's leg was
checked. Finding nothing glar-
ingly awry, he reentered the
game. X-rays the following day
revealed Brown had played the
entire contest against the Vikings
with a broken leg

During the off-season, Brown, driving home from a card game one night, got into an argument with a passenger who had lost big money. The guy pulled out a .22 revolver and shot Bob in the neck. Brown calmly drove himself to the hospital and had the wound dressed. The next year at training camp I told him that we were making a sign for his helmet that said, "How do you expect to stop me when a bullet couldn't?"

Domenic Gentile
on defensive tackle Bob Brown

On that drive, you became a man.

Vince Lombardi

to halfback Donny Anderson (1966–71), after Anderson's two gutsy pass receptions for first downs on the frozen turf of Lambeau Field, during the Packers' final drive of the Ice Bowl, helped set up Bart Starr's historic quarterback sneak for the game-winning touchdown on the final play of the 1967 NFL Championship Game against Dallas

When I arrived in New Orleans for the Super Bowl . . . I was supremely confident. I wasn't guaranteeing a victory like Joe Namath did with the New York Jets in 1969. I'm not really that kind of person but I am confident.

Brett Favre

The most amazing thing about Nitschke is that he played his entire career on one leg. His left leg had been injured so often in high school and college, the muscles had atrophied and they never fully regenerated. His left leg was 50 percent smaller in circumference than his right.

Domenic Gentile

Forrest Gregg and I talked about just hanging in there. Nothing was going to get you out of there. You play against the same guy and you say, "Hey, I don't care what happened last week, today we're going to go after it. The best man's going to win here, and I plan on being the best man."

Willie Davis

Ken was the kind of guy who could play in pain, which Lombardi, of course, admired. A couple days after one of his shoulder dislocations, he came into the locker room and demanded to be taped. Then he went out and hit the seven-man sled, as if nothing had happened. It was unbelievable. I think even Lombardi was surprised.

Domenic Gentile
on center Ken Bowman

I think many times we won football games because of our overall mental toughness. You play with an injury, broken fingers, sprained knees and ankles, and not only do you play, you go out and play well.

Willie Davis

Early in the game, Sam Huff drove [Jim] Taylor out of bounds, using his knees and elbows to full advantage as the two men skidded across the ice. Taylor struggled to his feet and leaned over, coughing blood. He wobbled back to the Packers huddle and told Starr to give him the ball again.

Bud Lea

author, at the outset of the 1962 NFL Championship Game at tundra-like Yankee Stadium, a brutal rematch between the Packers and New York Giants, taken by Green Bay 16–7, for its second consecutive league crown

VERNON J. BIEVER

Jim Taylor

Taylor isn't human. No human being could have taken the punishment he got today. Every time he was tackled it was like crashing him down on a concrete sidewalk because the ground was as hard as pavement. But he kept bouncing up, snarling at us and asking for more.

Sam Huff

New York Giants Hall of Fame linebacker (1956–63), after the 1962 NFL Championship Game

You look back and you know that you had nothing left—nothing—and yet you still continued to play. Like that Giants game. No one knows until they are faced with it just how much pain they can endure, how much suffering, how much effort they have left. That's the way it was that day.

> **Jim Taylor**
> *Hall of Fame fullback (1958–66), on the punishment he absorbed in the 1962 NFL title game*

Zeke Bratkowski, a very talented quarterback for many years, was always filled with a positive attitude and was prepared to step in when called upon. Several times in 1965, both during the regular season and playoffs, he had to perform in clutch situations after I sustained injuries. He was outstanding every time. This type of unselfishness, which ran through our veins, brought us our third championship of the Sixties, a victory over Cleveland.

Bart Starr

All the keys we must read are the science, and they are designed to get me close enough to play football. Then it's seek and destroy.

Dave Robinson
outside linebacker (1963–72)

This is the best win I ever had. It came so hard, all year long. Everything was hard. The season. The playoff [against Baltimore]. Everything. I never worked so hard in my life for anything.

Vince Lombardi
after the 23–12 NFL Championship Game win over Cleveland, in the snow and mud at Lambeau Field in 1965

He possesses a will that never takes "won't" for an answer.

Larry Weisman
sportswriter, USA Today, on Brett Favre, voted No. 1 in the newspaper's 10 Toughest Athletes list

PACKER HUMOR

Wonder of wonders, who do you think broke into the scoring summary? That sylph of 270 pounds, Calvin Hubbard!

Arch Ward

on the leviathan Hall of Fame tackle's second-half touchdown reception in Green Bay's 37–7 victory over the Staten Island Stapletons, Nov. 30, 1930, at Staten Island. Hubbard, usually a tackle, was listed as a starter at end for that game

When Coach Lombardi tells me to sit down, I don't even look for a chair.

Henry Jordan
Hall of Fame defensive tackle
(1959–69)

I wonder if the rumor is true that some TV stores in Wisconsin after the Super Bowl loss to Denver were selling used, dented television sets?

Daniel Edelstein

I may be a little old, but I can still run a hell of a lot better than you can see.

> **Tony Canadeo**
>
> *to an official who had noticed Canadeo's gray hair at the bottom of a pile and wondered if he might be too old to be playing football. Canadeo had premature gray hair since age 16*

My show will never challenge *Meet the Press* as a public affairs program . . . but each Wednesday evening, Don Hutson, the great former end of the Packers, one of my assistant coaches, and I go into that studio at WBAY-TV and try not to look and sound like the Three Stooges.

> **Vince Lombardi**

I was running around the field looking for people to hug. Just my luck, I found 300-pound guard Ron Hallstrom. I head-butted him with my helmet and split open my forehead.

Brett Favre

*on his first win at quarterback
for the Packers and Green Bay's
first win of the 1992 season,
a 24–23 come-from-behind win
against Cincinnati at Lambeau
Field on Sept. 20*

Brett's the kind of kid you would kick out of kindergarten.

Jerry Glanville

*former Houston Oilers/Atlanta
Falcons head coach; Favre's
mentor at Atlanta in 1991*

Playing quarterback in grade school, I didn't look the part. My helmet had a bar right down the middle like a linebacker's helmet. I looked like Ray Nitschke. In the seventh grade I took a hacksaw and cut the bar off. Enough of Nitschke, I wanted to look like Roger Staubach.

Brett Favre

In other cities, fans throw things at the players. In Green Bay, the players throw themselves at the fans.

Anonymous
on the Packers' pack of Lambeau Leapers, first popularized by wide receiver Robert Brooks

When people think of Reggie White, they think of this big man who's awesome and all-world on the field and a preacher off it. What they don't see is the guy who imitates Redd Foxx doing Fred Sanford, or Ali, or Bill Cosby. He's also a jokester. Reggie has the worst jokes in the world, but we all laugh because they're so bad.

Brett Favre

Coach Lombardi had planned to be here today, but he had a little accident while he was on vacation down in Miami. He was out for a morning stroll and got struck by a speedboat.

Bart Starr

LeRoy Butler, our strong safety, is what you'd call an instigator. . . . All those little dance steps and hand-jive and things that the team does on the field, that's all LeRoy. He is responsible for the whole deal. LeRoy should be listed in the program as our strong safety/dance choreographer.

Brett Favre

In a playoff game against the Los Angeles Rams, things were going so well that Coach Lombardi didn't even come into the locker room at halftime. Instead, he bought two hot dogs and two Cokes and went out and fed 50,000 people.

Bart Starr

I feel OK, but how's the crowd taking it?

Paul Hornung

upon being revived after he was knocked unconscious in a game while at Notre Dame

It's the Christian and the antichrist.

Sean Jones

on teammates Don Beebe and Jim McMahon, who were asked to address the team during the off week before Super Bowl XXXI. Moments earlier, Coach Mike Holmgren had presented the pair as "the little bad angel and the little good one." As the late sportswriter Dick Schaap said, "No one raised his hand to ask which was which"

As the struggle continued, one Packer after another was hurt—not injured, but hit, knocked down, dazed, bloodied. The little hurts Vince Lombardi says you have to play with if you want the championship badly enough. Huddling late in the game, the battered Bart Starr asked one receiver after another for a word of encouragement, but each reported he was hurting or too well covered. Finally Max McGee suggested, "Why don't you throw an incomplete pass and nobody will get hurt."

> **Phil Bengtson**
> *defensive coordinator under*
> *Vince Lombardi (1959–67)*
> *and head coach (1968–70)*

First time in five years my uniform has been dirty.

Don Chandler

punter/placekicker (1965–67), who drew a key fourth-quarter roughing-the-kicker penalty in the 1965 NFL title game against Cleveland, enabling the Packers to maintain possession of the ball

There was a sign in our locker room, and I think we all knew it related to our mission—stopping Jim Brown. It said, "Pursue the shortest course to the ball carrier. Arrive in bad humor."

Lionel Aldridge

defensive end (1963–71), before the 1965 NFL Championship Game against Cleveland

On the eve of Super Bowl XXXI, Max McGee told people he was going to stay out all night in New Orleans just to prove he could *broadcast* without sleep. McGee had proved he could *play* without sleep in Super Bowl I. The night before that game, which he was expecting to watch from the bench, he had snuck out after curfew to resume acquaintances with a blond young woman he had met only a few hours earlier. McGee had returned to the Packers' hotel roughly in time for breakfast.

Dick Schaap

McGee's partying skills had seriously eroded by 1997. At midnight, Paul Hornung informed Schaap, who was hosting a Super Bowl Eve party that both Hornung and McGee were attending, that he was leaving to take Max home and put him to bed. "It's past his bedtime," admitted Hornung, "and past mine, too."

Curly Lambeau, Cal Hubbard, Don Hutson, and Clarke Hinkle were four of the first five Packers elected to the Pro Football Hall of Fame. It's not hard to understand why they haven't named a boulevard after the fifth, Johnny Blood. [There is, however, a local beer named after him. You can get a glass of Johnny Blood Red at Titletown Brewery.]

Dick Schaap
late sportswriter/author/TV host
ESPN's The Sports Reporters

THE SCHOOL
OF LOMBARDI

Vince Lombardi, like Ben Hogan and golf, just knows something about his game that nobody else knows.

> **Jim Murray**
> *legendary sportswriter,*
> Los Angeles Times

*The statue of Vince Lombardi outside Lambeau Field
is a popular shrine among the Packer faithful.*

His nearsightedness may have hindered him, but for the most part his coaches and teammates thought he was a superior blocker precisely because he could hardly see. He hit opposing linemen a split second before he realized he was upon them, which gave him a reckless abandon, never holding back to cushion the blow.

David Maraniss

on Lombardi's playing days as one of Fordham's famed Seven Blocks of Granite

He was a driver. Not all the boys liked him, but he brought out the best in each of them.

Col. Earl "Red" Blaik

fabled Army head coach, on his assistant, Vince Lombardi (1949–53)

During his louder moments on the practice field, he could seem brutish, maniacal even; yet Lombardi usually knew where the line was that could not be crossed, where he would lose the respect of his players.

David Maraniss

His exhortations were counterbalanced by occasional hugs, unexpected pats on the back, and shared laughter—and also by his brainpower, which by football coaching standards was superior.

David Maraniss

You play this game with your power. You do what you do best—and you do it again and again.

Vince Lombardi

They call it coaching, but it is teaching. You do not just tell them it is so, but you show them the reasons why it is so, and you repeat and repeat until they are convinced, until they know.

Vince Lombardi

It sounded as though we were getting a foreign-type person. He was from New York.

> **John Ebert**
> *Green Bay merchant, on the*
> *hiring of Vince Lombardi in 1959*

The Green Bay Packahs.

> **Vince Lombardi**
> *in his native Brooklynese dialect*

We were making up our own notebooks at the time . . . just like his bible. I'd call mine my brains. I'd say I left my brains somewhere if I didn't have my notebook. It was Lombardi's brains.

John "Red" Cochran
offensive backfield coach, 1959–66, 1971–74; current college scout

I have never been associated with a loser, and I don't expect to be now.

Vince Lombardi
upon arriving in Green Bay, in 1959, to take over the Packers' head coaching job

We're not just going to start with a clean slate. We're going to throw the old slate away.

> ### Vince Lombardi
> *unfolding his first-year plan for the Packers*

Football is a symbol of what's best in American life. A symbol of courage, stamina, coordinated efficiency, and teamwork. It's a Spartan game, a game of sacrifice and self-denial, a violent game that demands discipline seldom found.

> ### Vince Lombardi

When you combine sincerity with sensitivity and intelligence, the individual tends to be tense.

Vince Lombardi

In this game, we're always looking for catch-phrases, especially with a connotation of masculinity.

Vince Lombardi

In pro ball it is to your advantage not to run to a specific hole but to run to daylight. . . . We school our backs to run to the daylight, wherever it is.

Vince Lombardi

Vince would tell us, "Boys, if you'll not settle for anything less than the best, you will be amazed at what you can do with your lives. You'll be amazed at how much you can rise in the world." I think this consistent unwillingness to settle for anything less than excellence was the greatest thing he left with people around him.

Bart Starr

Success is like a habit-forming drug: In victory, it saps your elation; in defeat it deepens your despair.

Vince Lombardi

You can't apologize for a score. It is up there on that board and nothing can change it now.

Vince Lombardi

If a man is running down the street with everything you own, you won't let him get away. That's tackling.

Vince Lombardi

There is nothing more demoralizing to a squad than to see the opposition run roughshod over you.

Vince Lombardi

For the most part, you only remember your losses.

Vince Lombardi

You defeat defeatism with confidence, and confidence comes from the man who leads. You just have it. It is not something you get. You have to have it right here in your belly.

Vince Lombardi

The satisfactions are few for perfectionists, but I have never known a good coach who wasn't one.

Vince Lombardi

I could not have played for anyone else than Vince. One of his first personnel moves was one of his smartest—he brought me to Green Bay. One of his last actions before leaving the Packers had an equally profound effect on my life—he called me in and told me to retire. So you can see how I lived and died with Lombardi.

Fuzzy Thurston

If Lombardi was on your case, that meant that he saw something in you. There was more reason to be concerned if he didn't yell at you; that usually meant you were a goner.

David Maraniss
paraphrasing an observation once made by Lombardi's wife, Marie

None of our injuries hurt him at all.

Jerry Kramer
on Lombardi's outlook on injuries, which he believed were a state of mind

He treats us all alike—like dogs.

Henry Jordan

Fatigue makes cowards of us all.

Vince Lombardi

His [Lombardi's] bronze bust at the Pro Football Hall of Fame in Canton, Ohio, has the shiniest nose, touched by more than any other by the faithful, the sporting world equivalent of rubbing St. Peter's foot in Rome.

David Maraniss

Winning isn't everything, but making the effort to win is.

Vince Lombardi

a correction voiced by Bart Starr on the oft-quoted Lombardi-ism: "Winning isn't everything; it's the only thing"

You might reduce Lombardi's coaching philosophy to a single sentence: In any game, you do the things you do best and you do them over and over and over.

George Halas

Chicago Bears founder/player/head coach

He always does an extremely fine job of getting us worked up. You could run through the wall when he lets you go. He doesn't plead. He just stands there telling us what to do in his very authoritative voice.

Bart Starr

Has this become a game for madmen and am I one of them?

Vince Lombardi

It was like watching the greatest Shakespearean character you have ever seen. . . . He laughed. He cried. He prayed. He motivated. He communicated with human emotions.

Chuck Lane

former Packers public relations director, on Lombardi

[C]urly] Lambeau was a triple-threat back. He ran and passed from the tailback position in the single wing and employed the now long forgotten art of drop-kicking for field goals and extra points.

John B. Torinus
*on Green Bay's three-time
All-Pro halfback (1922–24)
and future coaching legend*

The versatile Lambeau once tossed 45 passes in a game, completing 37.

[H]e liked to win above everything. He was a dedicated football man, a motivator. He had great ideas and was ahead of his time.

Tony Canadeo
on Curly Lambeau

[H]e was one of those rare coaches like Paul Brown or Vince Lombardi—he could see things in a ballplayer that other coaches couldn't.

Clarke Hinkle
on Lambeau

[I]'ve got all the emotions in excess and a hair-trigger controls them. I anger and I laugh and I cry quickly.

Vince Lombardi

[T]here isn't a day that goes by that I don't think of that man.

Willie Davis

[H]e could have made a success out of the Edsel.

Sonny Jurgensen
*Philadelphia Eagles/Washington
Redskins Hall of Fame
quarterback (1957–74),
on Lombardi*

Lombardi, a certain magic still lingers in the very name. It speaks of duels in the snow and the cold November mud.

John Facenda
legendary narrator,
the "Voice of God" of NFL Films

Perhaps we're living in Camelot. Many things have been said about Coach Lombardi, and he is not always understood by those who quote him. But the players understand. This is one beautiful man.

Jerry Kramer

Heart power is the strength of the Green Bay Packers.

Vince Lombardi

7

PACKER LEGENDS

Johnny Blood, now there's a guy! He was a rangy halfback, about 6–2 and 190, and had great speed. When he was 35 and Don Hutson was 24, he raced Hutson 100 yards. Hutson could outrun the wind, but he beat Johnny in that race by only a step. Johnny was the kind of guy who could read Shakespeare, Chaucer, and all those kind of people, although when he was drinking he would read filthy dime novels.

Clarke Hinkle
Hall of Fame fullback (1932–41),
as told to author/writer Myron Cope

Mike Michalske, Johnny Blood, Cal Hubbard, and Clarke Hinkle—to mention only a few—often remarked that Lambeau wasn't much of a field strategist, but he made up for it in other ways, mostly with hard work. . . . Unlike other National Football League coaches, Lambeau personally went looking for players all over the country instead of just reading about them in the newspapers.

Larry Names

Above all, Lambeau was a showman. Early on he recognized that professional football was as much an entertainment medium as it was a sports event.

John B. Torinus

Johnny Blood and a friend who shall forever be identified as Sand decided, in the fine whimsy of youth, to leave the cloisters of Notre Dame. The method of their exit involved Johnny's purchase of a motorcycle. They scooted off . . . and churned down the line to a small town whose local cinema was advertising an attraction called *Blood and Sand*. . . . McNally glanced at the marquee and said, "That's it! From now on you're Sand and I'm Blood."

Arch Ward
on the legend of how John McNally came to be known as Johnny Blood

In McNally's day, highly valued collegiate eligibility was maintained by assuming aliases when collegians doubled as pros for pay on Sundays.

The swift and elusive Blood came into his own on his native turf. . . . He became the most feared pass-catching back in the whole circuit.

Arch Ward

*on Johnny Blood's first year
with Green Bay, 1929—his
fourth team in his first five years
in the NFL*

Talk about swingers, what about Johnny Blood? One year, I played a couple of post-season exhibition games for Green Bay and roomed with Blood. What a guy! A couple of girls wanted Johnny to sign a program, and he said, "I'll do better than that. I'll sign it in blood." He cut his wrist with a knife and signed that program in blood, and he had to have about four stitches taken in the wrist. He was a lovable guy, a very learned guy, and one whale of a football player.

Red Grange

Arnie Herber could throw a football almost the length of the field. On some occasions, he would throw into the end zone instead of taking a chance punting on a slippery field, for in those days a pass on fourth down into the end zone came out to the 20-yard line.

John B. Torinus

Arnie Herber played quarterback from 1930 to 1940.

Herber had pudgy hands with short fingers that kept him from taking a normal grip on the ball. Instead of wrapping his hand around the pigskin, Herber let the ball rest on his palm. Instead of throwing the ball, he heaved it long distances with incredible accuracy.

Larry Names

Arnie Herber stood alone as the best long passer in the history of the game.

Larry Names

Prior to 1931, several All-Pro teams were selected each year, but none of them were considered official by the league. Finally, the NFL front office sanctioned a league all-star team to be voted on by the sportswriters of each NFL city. Lavvie Dilweg, Cal Hubbard, Mike Michalske, and Johnny Blood were chosen from the Packers. Blood also led the league in scoring with 78 points on 13 touchdowns.

Larry Names

During the '20s, the Packers had several great backs who played for them, but none really achieved the superstar status that Clarke Hinkle did in the '30s. Hinkle could do everything except pass. He could punt with anybody in the league. He was an excellent place-kicker, too. Above all, he was a power runner with speed.

Larry Names

Hinkle could pound a line and drive back the best defenders in the league, including the legendary Bronko Nagurski. Their famous head-to-head encounters have been told and retold for decades. . . . Hinkle and Nagurski played in a time of little padding and no face masks on leather helmets. When they met head-to-head, often only one of them got up for the next play.

Larry Names

Everyone in the stadium braced for the collision, a head-on at about the Bear 30. For a few minutes both players lay sprawled out on the field. Then Hinkle stumbled to his feet and staggered over to the sidelines. Nagurski was still prone. The Bears carried him off the field.

John B. Torinus

on the first meeting between Green Bay Packers Hall of Fame fullback Clarke Hinkle and Chicago Bears legend Bronko Nagurski, Sept. 25, 1932. The game played to a scoreless tie

He was the hardest runner I ever tried to tackle. When you hit him, it would just pop every joint all the way down to your toes.

Clyde "Bulldog" Turner

Chicago Bears Hall of Fame center/linebacker (1940–52), on Clarke Hinkle

Canadeo was an average-size back, but he had Hall of Fame desire.

Jerry Poling
author, on halfback
Tony Canadeo (1941–44, 1946–52)

For years while playing with the Packers, Tony was called the "Gray Ghost of Gonzaga. . . . During his sophomore year at Gonzaga he got the nickname the "Spokane Spook" from one of the sports-writers, who wrote that "he ran with a ghostly gallop." . . . Later on, "Spook" became "Ghost," and "Gray" was added.

David Zimmerman
author

If you closed your eyes you could imagine him, one fist clenched, shouting marching orders to linemen as he rounded a corner on a Packer sweep 50 years earlier. He was and still is a presence.

> **Jerry Poling**
> *on Hall of Famer Tony*
> *Canadeo, who died Nov. 30,*
> *2003, at age 84*

When Tony ran, he ran like a hoodlum. His right knee was raised up like he was going over a hurdle and his right foot would flatten out and the left foot would be his digging foot. His running style was kind of his own.

> **Damon Tassos**
> *guard (1947–49)*

Tony Canadeo

VERNON J. BIEVER

My right leg isn't quite sure what the left leg is going to do.

Tony Canadeo

Having the privilege of standing on the Packer sidelines, I was amazed at the explosive hitting on the field. In those days, players wore old leather helmets with no facemasks. Being so close to the action I could hear Canadeo screaming obscenities at the opponents as he carried the ball into the line. I think it was his way of releasing tension. But he'd just scream at them.

Earl Gillespie
popular 1950s Packers broadcaster

Tony Canadeo was reincarnated as the Gray Ghost of Green Bay. For more than half a century and parts of six decades, he influenced the fortunes of the Packers, first as a star player and then as a member of the team's executive committee. He was there in the 1940s, playing offense and defense, sans face mask, and buying Packer stock for himself and his children to help the financially troubled team. No one can claim a longer association with the Packers.

Jerry Poling

Like Lambeau, the name Canadeo has become synonymous with Packer football. Someday, something in Packerland will be named after him, a road like Canadeo Way or Canadeo Drive.

Jerry Poling

When I dream about the future and my place in the game, I think about how great it would be to have a street in Green Bay named after me. Favre Boulevard. That would be pretty cool. Although the way I drive, it might be safer to name a park after me.

Brett Favre

They'll probably name an alley after me.

Mike Holmgren

When I joined this club in 1959, he was more celebrated for his reputed exploits off the field than on, but after the months I had spent studying the movies of Packer games, I knew that one of the ballplayers I needed was Paul Hornung.

Vince Lombardi

Your quarterback days are over. You won't have to worry about playing three positions anymore. You are my left halfback. You're my Frank Gifford. You're either going to be my left halfback or you're not going to make it in pro football.

Vince Lombardi

in his initial phone call to Paul Hornung soon after taking the Packers head coaching job

VERNON J. BIEVER

Paul Hornung

Paul Hornung is one of those great money ballplayers. In the middle of the field he may be only slightly better than an average ballplayer, but inside that 20-yard line he is one of the greatest I've ever seen. He smells that goal line.

Vince Lombardi

Before our 1961 championship game, I was under the impression that Tom Moore could run as well as Paul Hornung and that Ben Agajanian could kick as well or better. But the week before the game, when Paul got that leave from the army and walked into that locker room, you could just feel the confidence grow in that room.

Henry Jordan

I did a book report in fifth grade on Paul Hornung. I probably got an A on it. When I met Hornung, I told him that. He seemed impressed.

Brett Favre

Jim Taylor runs best with somebody hanging on to him.

Henry Jordan

You gotta sting 'em a little. You've gotta make those tacklers respect you.

Jim Taylor

In an open field our James is something else again. When he sees a clear field ahead he hunts down somebody to run into, and while you have to enjoy body contact to play this game, Jimmy exults in it.

Vince Lombardi
on Jim Taylor

They respect him. In fact, every time he carries the ball there are 11 of them, all of whom want to pay their respects to him personally.

Vince Lombardi
on Jim Taylor

You're as tough as a rat!

Ray Nitschke
middle linebacker (1958–72), to Jim Taylor after Taylor's 161-yard rushing performance against San Francisco near the close of the 1960 season

He is not a bad blocker, but he would be a great one with his ruggedness, his quickness, and his agility, if they would just change the rules and let him carry a football while he's blocking.

Vince Lombardi
on Jim Taylor

Bart Starr established several NFL records during his phenomenal 16-year career, perhaps the most impressive of which was a streak of 294 consecutive pass attempts without an interception. . . . His career completion percentage was 57.4, at the time an NFL record. He led the league in passing three times [1962, '64 and '66], played in four Pro Bowls, and was the MVP of the first two Super Bowls. He threw for 23,718 yards and 152 touchdowns, despite the fact that Vince Lombardi's offense was run-oriented.

Domenic Gentile

When I joined this team the opinion around here and in the league was that Starr would never make it. They said he couldn't throw well enough and wasn't tough enough, that he had no confidence in himself and that no one had confidence in him.

Vince Lombardi

He is the son of an army master sergeant. He grew up on army posts and he still calls me "sir." When I first met him he struck me as so polite and so self-effacing that I wondered if maybe he wasn't too nice a boy to be the authoritarian leader that your quarterback must be.

Vince Lombardi
on Bart Starr

He was a superstar without a superstar's ego.

Domenic Gentile
on Bart Starr

Statistics are impressive only if they are the by-product of winning.

Bart Starr

There is no one on this team who is more conscientious and dedicated than Bart Starr.

Vince Lombardi

He was a master at baiting defenses. Nobody in the history of the game, before or since, was as effective throwing the ball off play-action fakes on third-down-and-short yardage situations.

Domenic Gentile

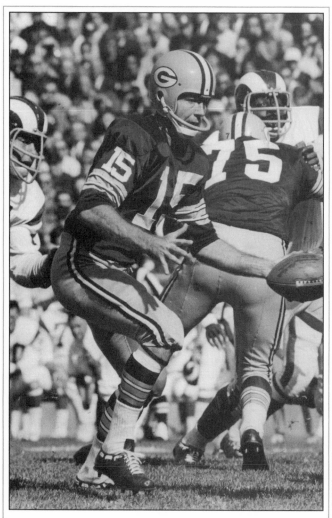

Vernon J. Biever

Bart Starr

He and Vince were hand and glove.

Murray Warmath
*fellow assistant coach with
Lombardi at West Point under
Red Blaik, on the Lombardi-
Starr relationship of coach
and quarterback*

God, Bart Starr, what he did during his career was unbelievable. I wish I could be half as good as he was. I keep a football autographed by Bart and myself on a shelf in my home office. I feel honored to have my name on the same ball as his.

Brett Favre

There have been many great quarterbacks in the NFL—Johnny Unitas, Terry Bradshaw, Joe Montana, Otto Graham, Sammy Baugh, Fran Tarkenton, Sid Luckman, Dan Marino, Joe Namath . . . the list goes on and on. I'd take Starr over all of them. In a heartbeat.

Domenic Gentile

Bart Starr is the greatest of all time.

Vince Lombardi

Willie Wood, a guy undersized in almost every dimension, many times lined up against the tight end. Willie just had no sense of backing off. I used to see him come up and hit Mike Ditka, Monte Clark, and other big tight ends, and he would hit 'em where they've been. He did it with more aggressiveness and more toughness than anybody.

Willie Davis

They were right about his height and lack of top speed, but what they didn't know is that he can jump like a gazelle. He is the most natural defensive back we have.

Vince Lombardi
on Willie Wood

Pro football has been the difference between me being just another guy and having something today. I was from just a small Negro school [Grambling], and I sometimes shake when I think I might not have finished college and not made a pro club.

Willie Davis

What Forrest Gregg loved to do most was get beyond the line of scrimmage and rumble downfield, setting his radar on a linebacker to eliminate. In time, Lombardi would come to regard his square-jawed right tackle as the greatest downfield blocker he had ever seen.

David Maraniss

Quarterbacks will tell you who gives them the most trouble. They'll tell you who really makes them eat that football. It's people like Ray Nitschke and Sam Huff. They're the best in my book.

Dick Butkus
Chicago Bears Hall of Fame linebacker

Ray kind of annihilates you when he makes a tackle. That's his style, just like Butkus. You're not supposed to be a nice guy out there. Ray just does it with a little more vim and vigor.

Ed O'Bradovich
defensive end, Chicago Bears (1962–71), on Ray Nitschke

No one got punished more and no one punished in return more than Ray Nitschke.

Willie Davis

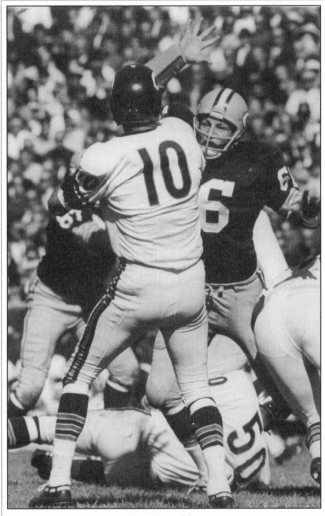

Ray Nitschke

VERNON J. BIEVER

Herb Adderley was basically an intimidator. I would say there were very few split receivers who wanted to catch the ball in front of Herb.

Willie Davis

Jerry Kramer and Forrest Gregg are two names that would definitely be on my "toughness" team. Gregg, there were times when a lesser person would have come out of the game, but he would suck it up and stay in there. It was almost like it was part of a code that we owed to each other. "Boy, if there's any way you can be out there, 'cause you're important to this thing." We lived with that.

Willie Davis

I'll take him at 75 percent over anyone else in the league.

Brett Favre
on Reggie White

VERNON J. BIEVER

Reggie White

When he runs onto the field, the field automatically tilts in your favor.

Ron Wolf
on Brett Favre

In 1992, Packers General Manager Ron Wolf made the bold move to send a first-round pick to the Atlanta Falcons for their third-string quarterback. Wolf received hate mail for his trouble, but he stood by his man.

Ron Havel
*on Wolf's acquisition of
quarterback Brett Favre*

The mark of a truly great player is that he makes the other players around him look a little bit better. Brett has that kind of quality about him.

Curley Hallman
head football coach during Favre's sophomore through senior seasons at Southern Mississippi

Brett Favre's got a fire in the pit of his stomach. He's as tough as they come. He makes mistakes, but he also makes plays, and that's the mark of a great quarterback.

Domenic Gentile

VERNON J. BIEVER

Brett Favre

From a young age I knew I had something pretty special in my right arm. When I was in grade school and at Dad's football practice, I'd be on the sidelines throwing as far as the high school quarterback. I knew that I had something that other kids didn't. I used to dream that my arm would take me somewhere special someday.

Brett Favre

Here is Favre throwing jump passes, something that hasn't been done since Sammy Baugh.

John Madden
former Oakland Raiders head coach and current Monday Night Football *analyst, on Brett Favre's occasional fakes without the ball after a handoff*

Brett Favre will compete with you until the end and do what it takes to win. He puts the team ahead of himself and before his stats.

> **John Elway**
> *Denver Broncos Hall of Fame*
> *quarterback (1983–98)*

He plays the game the way it's supposed to be played. You've got to play to win. He's a tough kid. He plays hurt. He's got a lot of confidence in himself. Yeah, he reminds me of myself a bit.

> **Jim McMahon**
> *quarterback (1995–96),*
> *on Brett Favre*

SHRINE TO NO. 14

No one player has ever dominated the National Football League so thoroughly and convincingly as did the immortal Don Hutson during the 11-year period he demoralized opponents' defenses, from 1935 to '45.

John B. Torinus

Until I started receiving letters from Curly Lambeau, I had given no thought at all to playing pro football. None at all. I'd never heard of the Green Bay Packers. Down in Alabama there was nothing in the papers about pro football. They didn't even have the results in the papers.

Don Hutson
legendary Hall of Fame end (1935–45), who at one time held every significant NFL pass-receiving record

Don Hutson was to professional football what Babe Ruth was to major league baseball and Michael Jordan was to the National Basketball Association.

Larry Names

I saw Herber throw this pass downfield, and I saw this lanky guy loping down toward me. I knew the ball was going way over my head, and I was sure it was way out of Hutson's reach. But all of a sudden, he turned on his speed, ran right by me, took the pass in perfect stride, and went on for a touchdown.

Beattie Feathers

Chicago Bears halfback/safety, who was victimized on the first play from scrimmage in Green Bay's second game of 1935 (Sept. 22), reputedly the first pass thrown to Don Hutson in the NFL. That play was the ball game, as the Packers edged the Bears, 7–0

With only three minutes to play, the score was Bears 14, Packers 3. Hutson, out in the flat, took a pass from Herber and eluded all 11 Chicago Bears on his way to the goal line, making the score 14–10 with less than a minute left. On their first play from scrimmage, the Bears handed off to Bronko Nagurski, but Packer tackle Ernie Smith met him head-on, straightened him up, and stripped him of the ball. Smith also recovered. On the next play, Herber unloaded a bomb, found Hutson in the corner of the end zone, and the Packers won 17–14. The Hutson legend had been born.

John B. Torinus

on the return match against Chicago, Oct. 27, 1935, at Wrigley Field, during Hutson's rookie season

Don Hutson's rookie year contract, in 1935, was so large that Packer officials set up two bank accounts to keep the Alabama star's salary of $175 per game a secret in depression-era Green Bay.

Don Davenport

Not only did he have the great change of pace, but he also had the greatest pair of hands of any end who ever played the game.

John B. Torinus

In 1939, in the NFL title game played at State Fair Park in Milwaukee, the Packers whitewashed the New York Giants, 27–0. Surprisingly, Hutson did not score in that game, spending most of the afternoon acting as a decoy for the other ends.

John B. Torinus

Don Hutson

VERNON J. BIEVER

Don Hutson had flat feet and had to have his feet taped in a special way for football. That explains his peculiar loping running style, which completely baffled opponents. He never seemed to be running as fast as he really was.

Jim Ford

collector of Packers trivia,
as told to John B. Torinus

All along George Halas had said he feared Don Hutson more than any other player in the NFL. Hutson was such a game-breaker that Halas designed special defenses just for him, and each one of them called for two Bears to cover him. Even so, Hutson often broke into the clear and caught the ball. Halas also said, in so many words, that without Hutson, the Packers were just another team.

Larry Names

Hutson is so extraordinary that I concede him two touchdowns a game and just hope we can score more.

George Halas

Because he was the premier receiver of his time, Hutson was double- or triple-teamed by every defense he went up against after his first year in the league. That made his single-game record [since broken] of 14 catches against the New York Giants in 1942 all the more remarkable.

Larry Names

If [Cecil] Isbell had stayed in the game instead of turning to coaching, he and Hutson would have had one field day after another against the war-time replacement players of the NFL.

Larry Names

He terrorized defensive backs merely stepping onto the field.

John B. Torinus

Hutson's most astounding marks for one quarter were those he set against the Lions in Green Bay in 1945, when he caught four TD passes and booted five PATs for a total of 29 points in the second period of that game. Even in a later age when passing became much more dominant in the pro game, no one would catch four touchdown passes or score 29 points in a single quarter.

Larry Names

Hutson was the first Packer to have his jersey retired. His No. 14 was retired during a ceremony at old City Stadium in 1951. He was also an original inductee into the Pro Football Hall of Fame in 1963 and the Packer Hall of Fame.

Larry Names

Any comparison of Hutson's feats must be tempered with one very important factor: The NFL season was only 11 games long when Hutson played. Taking that point into consideration, one wonders what sort of marks he would have set if he had played 16-game seasons. Certainly his achievements rank with those of all-time greats in any other sport.

John B. Torinus

During Hutson's 11 seasons in Green Bay, the Packers played six 11-game seasons, three 10-game seasons, and two 12-game seasons.

If anyone ever exemplified what it means to be a Packer on and off the field and in life after football, it was Don Hutson.

Larry Names

TALES FROM THE TUNDRA

As long as people pay attention to pro football, they will talk about what happened on New Year's Eve, 1967, at Lambeau Field.

Bud Lea

on Green Bay's dramatic 21–17 win over Dallas in the 1967 NFL Championship Game, the legendary Ice Bowl

They will remember the Packers driving on the frozen tundra with fewer than five minutes remaining. . . . They will remember Bart Starr scoring the winning touchdown on a daring quarterback sneak at the end of the game. . . . And surely, they will remember the weather—the coldest New Year's Eve in Green Bay's cold history.

Bud Lea

It's just too cold to play. They're gonna call this game off. They're not going to play in this.

Willie Wood

waiting for a tow truck to start his car the morning of the Ice Bowl, Dec. 31, 1967

Dallas Cowboys defensive linemen Bob Lilly and George Andrie were roommates. When Lilly awoke, Andrie had already dressed and gone to an early Mass. . . . Then Andrie came back and didn't say anything about the temperature outside. He got a glass of water, pulled back the curtain and threw the water on the window. The water froze before it ran down to the windowsill.

Bud Lea
on the morning of the Ice Bowl

Good afternoon, ladies and gentlemen, and welcome to the National Football League championship at Green Bay, Wisconsin. . . . The temperature is 13 degrees below zero.

Frank Gifford
CBS broadcaster,
his 1967 league title game
introduction to a national
television audience

There was this incredible haze of breath, tens of thousands of puffs coming out, like seeing big buffaloes in an enormous herd on the winter plains. It was prehistoric.

> **Gary Knafelc**
> *end (1954–62), on the Ice Bowl*
> *crowd at Lambeau Field,*
> *Dec. 31, 1967*

Players said it was as if someone had taken a stucco wall and laid it on the ground. Clumps of mud had coagulated and stuck to the rock-hard ground.

> **David Maraniss**
> *on the condition of Lambeau*
> *Field prior to the Ice Bowl*

It made AstroTurf feel like a pillow.

Chuck Mercein
fullback (1967-69),
on icy Lambeau Field

Mercein made key plays on the Packers' final drive, including a 19-yard reception and an 8-yard ramble to the 3-yard line that helped set up Bart Starr's famous, game-winning quarterback sneak.

The Cowboys looked like earthmen on Mars, the outfits they wore. Most of them had hooded sweatshirts on underneath their helmets, which looked silly as hell. And a kind of scarf thing around their faces with their eyes cut out. They looked like monsters in a grade B movie.

Chuck Mercein
on the Packers' Ice Bowl
opponents

The question ultimately is whether anyone can survive playing in these conditions.

Willie Davis
before the Ice Bowl

It was like playing in a meat locker.

Chuck Mercein

No gloves.

Vince Lombardi
to his Green Bay Packers squad
before the start of the Ice Bowl

My dad and I went to the Ice Bowl, but we spent most of the game huddling in the most popular place in Lambeau Field: the men's restroom. It was our refuge from the frigid elements that had dropped the temperature to minus-13 degrees at kickoff. Inside the restroom, I tried listening to the championship game on my portable transistor radio. No luck. It was frozen, just like my feet and hands.

Daniel Edelstein

Three to one it breaks when he kicks it.

Bob Woessner

Press-Gazette *writer,*
as Green Bay's Don Chandler
approached the ball on the
opening kickoff of the Ice Bowl

You can't catch a pass with your hands in your pants. We played 11 guys against 10 whenever he did that. He was just stone cold.

Tom Brown

strong safety (1964–68),
on Dallas Cowboys wide receiver
Bob Hayes during the Ice Bowl

Hayes tipped off every Cowboys offensive play by inadvertently tucking his hands inside his pants on running plays, pulling them out whenever Dallas passed.

Gentlemen, this man is like a son to me.

Vince Lombardi
*speaking of Paul Hornung to the
press corps prior to the Ice Bowl*

*Hornung had planned to watch the game from the press
box in relative warmth, but Lombardi insisted that he
join him on the sidelines. Hornung, scheduled for a halftime interview with CBS, was so cold he couldn't move
his mouth, and the interview had to be cancelled.*

The first band member to put a metal
mouthpiece to his mouth was the trombone player, and he pulled his lip off.

Tom Brookshier
*CBS color analyst and sideline
reporter at the Ice Bowl*

*With the wind chill factor falling to 40 degrees below
zero, the halftime show featuring the Wisconsin State
University of La Crosse marching band was cancelled.
While practicing that morning, several band members
had collapsed from the cold.*

That was the only game in my career in which I can honestly say I was wishing it would just hurry up and be over. . . . All I wanted to do was get inside and get warm. I took my foot and put it in front of one of those big ol' kerosene heaters, and even though I smelled leather, I never felt anything. My shoe was burning, but I couldn't feel anything. You could not run around fast enough to get warm. You couldn't run or cut or anything. You just tried to get in each other's way. A doctor told me a few years ago that my lungs were probably burned that day from the cold air.

Ralph Neely
Dallas Cowboys tackle
(1965–77), on Ice Bowl
conditions

Bill Schliebaum, the line judge, had his whistle freeze to his lips and lost a layer of skin yanking it loose.

David Maraniss

In the press box the windows were freezing up, making it almost impossible for the writers to see the game. Members of the press box crew were sent to a Mobil station across the street from the stadium to buy cans of antifreeze. They squirted the antifreeze on the top of the press box windows, and when it started running down it melted the frost.

Bud Lea
on working conditions at
Lambeau Field during the
Ice Bowl

I think I'll take another bite of my coffee.

Frank Gifford
CBS commentator for the
Ice Bowl

Ray Nitschke refused to go near the blowers—he had a tradition of kneeling on one knee near the coach when the defense was off the field—and now [in the third quarter] he was starting to get frostbite in his toes.

David Maraniss

The field was like a marble tabletop.

Bart Starr
down in the shadows of the
scoreboard, where Green Bay
was just one yard out from the
end zone, prior to his game-
winning quarterback sneak

Lombardi said he had never seen a worse day for football.

> **Bud Lea**
> *on the 1962 NFL title game*
> *—Green Bay vs. New York—*
> *at Yankee Stadium*

The temperature dipped from 20 at game time to 17 at the half to 10 at the end. What made it unbearable was the incessant wind. Forty-mile-per-hour gusts exploded across the frozen stadium, whipping an acre of dirt and debris into a swirling storm. Newspapers and trash blew across the field. The teams' benches were blown over. Occasionally a fan's hat would blow on the field. Once, the hat belonged to Lombardi.

> **Bud Lea**
> *on the '62 championship game*
> *at Yankee Stadium*

Those who played in it remember it as the coldest game they had ever played—colder than even the Ice Bowl game five years later in sub-zero Green Bay.

Bud Lea

*on the NFL Championship
Game at Yankee Stadium
in 1962*

The grassless field was like concrete . . . hard, frozen in large swatches, with holes and ruts everywhere. The stiff winds blew straight across the field. Yet from time to time, the two large flags on the poles in centerfield whipped straight out in opposite directions. That was how tricky the wind was.

Bud Lea

*on surface and wind conditions
at Yankee Stadium for the '62
title game*

The championship overshadows my getting 1,000 yards for the second year in a row. I wasn't aware of 1,000. I was thinking of getting first downs, eating up the clock, and getting closer to that goal line.

John Brockington
*running back (1971–77), on
his and the Packers' achievements
on Dec. 10, 1972, in the
minus-18-degree-wind-chill-factor
weather at frigid Metropolitan
Stadium in Minneapolis, where
Green Bay clinched the NFC
Central Division title with a
23–7 victory over the Vikings*

FAMOUS
MOMENTS

It was probably the most famous play in the most famous game ever played. And only one of the 11 guys who ran it knew what was going on.

Ken Bowman

center (1964–73), on Bart Starr's game-winning quarterback sneak in the Packers' 1967 NFL Championship Game win over Dallas—the legendary Ice Bowl

Cushions went flying in the air, while soaring hats were as thick as Green Bay flies on a July night. Staid gray-haired businessmen jumped around like school kids, and there was one continual din that could be heard for blocks away.

> **Anonymous Green Bay Press-Gazette reporter**
> *after the Packers won their 1921 season opener at Hagemeister Park against the Minneapolis Marines, 7–6, Oct. 23, 1921— the Packers' first game in the NFL*

In 1928, the little town of Green Bay first made its big splurge on the national sports scene, when the Packers beat the New York Giants at the Polo Grounds, 7–0, making headlines in all the metropolitan press.

> **John B. Torinus**

I was given two of the greatest thrills of my life last night and tonight by the welcome tendered by Green Bay fans, and I know every other member of the team feels the same as I do. When a city responds as it has done to our efforts, I'll say it certainly deserves a championship.

Curly Lambeau
after 20,000 Green Bay fans greeted the Packers upon their return from Chicago, where they defeated the Bears in the final game of the 1929 season to finish 12–0–1 to claim their first NFL championship

The Packers played the Boston Redskins in the world championship game in 1936, which was the only title game ever played on a neutral field, namely the Polo Grounds in New York, because Redskins owner George Marshall was in the process of moving his team to Washington due to poor attendance in the Massachusetts city. The Packers recovered a fumble at midfield immediately after the kickoff, and Herber dropped back and threw a 43-yard touchdown pass to Hutson, as the Packers completely dominated the Easterners, 21–6.

John B. Torinus

Not until 1933, when the Packers went 5–7–1, did they record their first losing season in franchise history.

Don Davenport

Our boys gave the Giants the best going-over they have ever taken, I'll bet.

Cecil Isbell

quarterback (1938–42), after the Packers' decisive 27–0 waxing of New York in the 1939 NFL Championship Game, at State Fair Park in Milwaukee, the first shutout ever in a league title game

Three Giants patrolled the lean Arkansan as he broke to his right. Too late did they realize their mistake. Irv Comp, carrying out the Hutson deception, was protected well enough to wheel and throw the ball to Fritsch, moving down the opposite side of the field in what amounted to privacy. Ted caught it on the New York 13-yard line and walked over.

Arch Ward

on the deciding touchdown in Green Bay's 14–7 win over the New York Giants in the 1944 NFL Championship Game

It just wouldn't have been appropriate if we hadn't won.

> **Billy Howton**
> *end (1952–58), on Green Bay's 21–17 win over the Bears that christened the opening of the new City Stadium (later renamed Lambeau Field), Sept. 29, 1957. Howton contributed to the celebration, pulling in eight receptions for 165 yards and a 38-yard touchdown pass from Babe Parilli*

It was like being run over by a Mack truck. . . . There were Packer tire tracks all over City Stadium.

> **Bud Lea**
> *on Green Bay's complete domination of the New York Giants in the 1961 NFL Championship Game*

They came in swinging from the heels, with fists and forearms and elbows. It was the most awesome thing I've ever been involved in. We had no way to stop them. They were like wild men. It was unending. They constantly punished us.

> **Greg Larson**
> *New York Giants*
> *center/guard/tackle (1961–73),*
> *on being butchered 37–0 by*
> *the Packers in the 1961 NFL*
> *title game*

Lombardi started taking his starters out in the fourth quarter out of respect for the Maras. He didn't want to rub it in.

> **Bud Lea**
> *on Green Bay's 1961 NFL*
> *Championship Game blowout*
> *of the New York Giants, whom*
> *Lombardi had served as offensive*
> *coordinator prior to coming to*
> *Green Bay*

It was a tremendous team effort all around by both units. Today Paul Hornung was a great, great player. He picked us up and did a terrific job.

Vince Lombardi
on Hornung's MVP performance in the 1961 NFL Championship Game

I was just ready to play. I wanted us to score 70 points on them, but Vince didn't. We could've scored 70 points that day.

Paul Hornung
on the 37–0 whitewashing of New York in the 1961 NFL title game

That one [the 37–0 title game loss to Green Bay in 1961] really stings. It was the low point of my career. It burned into my brain, and the only way I can get rid of the memory is by returning the aggravation. If we win this game it won't be enough. We have to destroy the Packers and Lombardi. It's the only way we can atone for what happened to us last year.

Andy Robustelli

New York Giants defensive end (1956–64), on the eve of the 1962 NFL Championship Game rematch between Green Bay and New York at Yankee Stadium

Players couldn't catch passes or field punts because the ball danced without reason or pattern through the gusts. When Bart Starr and Y. A. Tittle tried to throw, the ball would start blowing back to them.

Bud Lea

on playing conditions at Yankee Stadium for the 1962 league title match between Green Bay and New York, won by the Packers, 16–7

[It] was one of the most violent of all NFL championship games. A game billed as a grudge match for the 1961 title game that ended in a quest for survival. If they had fought this one in a bar, the cops would have stopped it.

Bud Lea

on the 1962 NFL title game in New York

Probably the biggest moment in my career was the final field goal when we sealed the victory. All the guys were jumping on me. For an offensive guard, that doesn't happen.

Jerry Kramer

after kicking three field goals in the 1962 NFL title game under trying weather conditions

Wide by three feet.

Lou Michaels

Baltimore Colts tackle (1964–69), on Don Chandler's infamous 27-yard, game-tying field goal that sent the 1965 Western Conference playoff against Baltimore into overtime. Chandler's 25-yard field goal won it at 13:39 into overtime, allowing Green Bay to advance to the NFL Championship Game against Cleveland

The next year, the league extended the uprights 20 feet above the crossbar. They were called the Chandler Extension.

Bud Lea

on the aftermath from Don Chandler's controversial game-tying field goal in the Western Conference Playoff, Dec. 26, 1965, won by the Packers 13–10 in overtime

I held for kickers for years. I'd like to think I had a very good view of it. I didn't see any problem. I don't know what all the stir was about.

Bart Starr

holder on the questionable Chandler field goal

When Bart didn't get up, I knew I was going in. All I remember is that I thought that now it's all up to me, all the responsibility and all the money and the championship . . . all mine. My stomach began to churn.

Zeke Bratkowski
quarterback (1963–68, 1971), whose 22–of–39 passing performance for 248 yards in relief of injured Bart Starr in the 1965 Western Conference Playoff against the Baltimore Colts helped guide Green Bay to a 13–10 overtime victory and a berth in the following week's NFL Championship Game against Cleveland

During the 1965 season, "the Brat" saved four games substituting for Starr.

You know that pass that Jim Brown dropped in the end zone? He had it in his hands but Nitschke was all over him, just hustling and hollering and screaming after him.

Bob Skoronski

on the Cleveland fullback's third-quarter miscue in the 1965 NFL Championship Game, won by Green Bay 23–12. The Browns' Hall of Famer was held to 50 yards rushing

What the Browns needed was a Brown County snowplow, a bazooka, or a brick wall: something that could stop two runaway beer trucks. That's how Hornung and Taylor looked to the Browns.

Bud Lea

on the Packer duo's performances in the 1965 NFL Championship Game win over Cleveland. Hornung amassed 105 yards on 18 carries, Taylor 96 yards on 27 rushes. Hornung also added a 13-yard, third-quarter scoring sweep to seal the victory

Carroll Dale's most memorable catch with the Packers was in the 1965 NFL Championship Game. He went into the huddle and told Bart Starr to throw it long, because the defensive back was playing him tight. Dale ran straight up the field on a fly pattern. Bart underthrew the ball a little, but Carroll adjusted, came back for it, then turned the defender around with a great fake. It was one of those plays where, as you watch it develop, you have absolutely no doubt that it is going to go for a touchdown.

Domenic Gentile

on Dale's 47-yard touchdown reception to open the scoring in the 1965 NFL Championship Game

My feet never touched the ground. I floated back to the sidelines.

> **Jim Grabowski**
>
> *fullback (1966–70), on his 18-yard scoring return of a Mel Renfro kickoff-return fumble that gave Green Bay a 14–0 first quarter lead over Dallas in the 1966 NFL title game*

A mere two yards stood between Dallas turning the game into a tie. But against the Packers' defense, those two yards might as well have been two miles.

> **Bud Lea**
>
> *on the Dallas Cowboys' final offensive thrust of the 1966 NFL title game: first and goal on the 2-yard line, with Green Bay holding on to a 34–27 lead*

We were leading, 34–27, and Dallas had a first down on the 2-yard line. We were terrified. All we could do was pray. We hadn't stopped the Cowboys all afternoon. They had the momentum and we were emotionally exhausted. Then somebody in the Cowboys line [left tackle Jim Boeke] jumped offside and we were saved. We won that game because of Vince Lombardi. Lombardi discipline was the difference. Nobody who played for Lombardi would have ever jumped offside and cost the club a ballgame or a championship. He wouldn't have permitted it.

> ### Max McGee
>
> *wide receiver/punter (1954, 1957–67), on the shocking turn of events influencing the outcome of the 1966 NFL Championship Game, Green Bay vs. Dallas, in the Cotton Bowl, Jan. 1, 1967*

I got a good grip on [Don] Meredith's left arm and part of his right arm when he got rid of the ball. I got sick to my stomach when he got the pass off. The first thing I heard was the crowd. I jumped up and saw Tom Brown getting up with the ball.

Dave Robinson

on the Dallas Cowboys' final offensive play of the 1966 NFL Championship Game, won by Green Bay, 34–27

Tom Brown, the Packers' strong safety, grabbed the football like a superhero catching a baby to preserve Green Bay's 34–27 victory. The catch shocked 75,000.

Bud Lea

on Brown's 1966 NFL title game-ending interception of Don Meredith's desperation end-zone pass

The showdown between the Green Bay Packers and the Kansas City Chiefs was called the AFL-NFL World Championship Game. Not the Super Bowl. The game got huge television coverage because one of the terms of the merger was that CBS, which carried NFL games, and NBC, which showed the AFL, both got to carry this one. Each team used its own league ball on offense. This was the strangest of all championship games.

Bud Lea
on the first Super Bowl,
Jan. 15, 1967

Pour it on, boys. There will be a lot more when we tear apart the NFL.

Hank Stram

Kansas City Chiefs Hall of Fame head coach, in the closing minutes of the Chiefs' 31–7 rout of the Buffalo Bills in the 1966 AFL Championship Game. Stram then optimistically began looking forward to his as-yet-undetermined NFL opponent in the first Super Bowl

Lombardi was on edge all week. He was carrying the weight of the entire NFL. . . . He didn't know much about the Chiefs. He just knew he was expected to put a whipping on them.

Bud Lea

on the buildup to Super Bowl I

Bart hit third-down after third-down pass to Max McGee because they covered the strong side and Max was just standing there. Bart just threw and threw and threw to him.

Zeke Bratkowski

on wide receiver McGee's stand-out performance in Super Bowl I

Max should have been named player of the game. I told Bart [MVP] that a hundred times, and he agreed with me. That was the greatest performance by a guy who was out of shape. If Max had not been such a great athlete, he would never have done what he did.

Paul Hornung

on McGee's seven catches, 138 receiving yards, and two touchdowns in Super Bowl I

Adding to the awesomeness of McGee's performance is the well-documented story that he was out all night partying until 7:30 a.m. the morning of the Super Bowl.

This is it. We're going in.

> **Bart Starr**
> *in the huddle before the Packers'*
> *final drive of the 1967 NFL*
> *Championship Game, trailing*
> *Dallas 17–14 on their own 32*
> *with 4:50 remaining*

The feeling I had was that we are going to score. Everyone in the huddle was calm. I didn't sense any anxiety or desperation. Determination, yes, but not desperation. Bart said just a few words, but he had this tremendous presence. He was the on-field personification of Lombardi.

> **Chuck Mercein**
> *on the final drive of the Ice Bowl*

I'm psyched, I want this thing to go right. I'm taking off and—lo and behold, Bart's not giving me the ball! He's kept it and he's in the end zone.

Chuck Mercein

on Starr's classic sneak behind the blocks of Jerry Kramer and Ken Bowman to win the 1967 NFL Championship Game, 21–17, over Dallas

On the final play, Mercein was supposed to get the ball, but Starr, while calling the count at the line of scrimmage, suddenly feared that Mercein might slip and not get to the hole. Starr's timeless end-zone dive was spontaneously improvised.

The coach, it could be said, had nothing to do with that final drive in a game that would be remembered thereafter as the Ice Bowl. Starr called the plays and scored the touchdown, Anderson and Mercein made key runs and catches, Kramer and Bowman threw crucial blocks. Yet that final drive . . . was the perfect expression of Vince Lombardi.

David Maraniss

The frozen tundra boiled down to one quarterback who was dangerously sure of himself. The Packers won, 21–17. They were NFL champions again, for an unprecedented third time in a row.

Bud Lea
on the Ice Bowl, the 1967 NFL Championship Game at Lambeau Field

I've been in Green Bay 10 years and I've never seen anybody tackle Fran Tarkenton three times in one game, but Big Cat did it today.

Dave Robinson
after defensive end Clarence Williams's (1970–77) stellar performance against Minnesota's future Hall of Fame quarterback, Dec. 10, 1972—a 23–7 Green Bay victory for the NFC Central Division crown

My first year there I managed to lead us to a last-second victory over Cincinnati. I hit Kitrick Taylor on a 35-yard touchdown with 13 seconds to play. We won, 24–23, and the fans in Lambeau went crazy. Walking off the field, I knew I'd have to be dead before I'd ever come out of the lineup again.

Brett Favre
Sept. 20, 1992

Somebody had to make the play, and somebody did.

Reggie White
whose fourth-down sack of John Elway preserved Green Bay's 30–27 win over Denver, Oct. 10, 1993. The victory turned around the 1–3 Packers, who then took seven of their next 11 games to reach the playoffs for the first time since 1982. It was White's second successive sack and third of the game

I've been here 25 years. This is the biggest moment I can remember.

Bob Harlan
Packers president (1989–), after Green Bay's 27–17 victory over the San Francisco 49ers in the 1995 NFC Divisional Playoffs at 3Com (Candlestick) Park

I haven't felt like this since Michigan.

Desmond Howard

punt/kick returner (1996, 1999), whose 71-yard first-quarter punt return for a touchdown ignited the Packers' 35–14 NFC Divisional Playoff victory at Lambeau Field over San Francisco for the second straight year, Jan. 4, 1997. Howard's remark referenced his Heisman Trophy-winning days at Ann Arbor

The place went wild. It was like a state of euphoria. It was colder than hell, and I looked around and nobody was leaving. Our fans wanted that moment to last forever no matter what the temperature was. It was a total celebration. The Super Bowl and this game were two different games. In some ways, the championship was more fun. Everybody got to celebrate with us.

Brett Favre

*on the Packers' 30–13 win
over the Carolina Panthers in the
1996 NFC Championship Game*

Here I was, living a dream, and it was everything I thought it would be. Best of all we won. It was a huge relief. If I never win another Super Bowl, at least I can say I won one. It was something that a lot of great quarterbacks have never done.

Brett Favre

on his 14–of–27 passing performance for 246 yards and two touchdowns in Green Bay's 35–21 victory over New England in Super Bowl XXXI

I got an early Christmas gift. It fell in my hands. Who said football was all skill?

Antonio Freeman
*wide receiver (1995–2001,
2003–), on the Immaculate
Deflection, the Brett Favre aerial
that bounced twice off Minnesota
corner Cris Dishman before
Freeman grabbed it while on the
ground himself. The Packer
wideout then scrambled to his feet
and averted another defender
before taking it into the end zone,
giving Green Bay a miraculous
26–20 overtime win over the
Vikings, Nov. 6, 2000*

THE ALL-TIME
GREEN BAY PACKERS TEAM

*O*h, there may be arguments aplenty: Starr over Favre? Lombardi over Lambeau?

Hinkle a linebacker? Johnny Blood taking one of the three receiver spots! Such are the thankless obstacles strewn about the course when one sets out to name an all-time team. At serious issue is fairness—to all eras. To my mind, it's unthinkable to pass over a Hinkle or a Blood just because they played in pre-modern times. As 60-minute men—and Hall of Famers—they deserve recognition.

And while Brett Favre can run circles around Bart Starr in terms of physical skills and stats, Starr, a two-time Super Bowl MVP with the highest postseason passer rating in NFL history (104.8), played with a consistency that even Favre would envy.

So, buckle up, Cheeseheads. Let's surf through the all-time greats of Packerland.

ALL-TIME PACKERS TEAM

Offense

DON HUTSON, *wide receiver*
CAL HUBBARD, *tackle*
MIKE MICHALSKE, *guard*
JIM RINGO, *center*
JERRY KRAMER, *guard*
FORREST GREGG, *tackle*
STERLING SHARPE, *wide receiver*
BART STARR, quarterback
JOHNNY BLOOD, *receiver/halfback*
PAUL HORNUNG, *running back*
JIM TAYLOR, *running back*

Defense

REGGIE WHITE, *defensive end*
HENRY JORDAN, *defensive tackle*
DAVE "HAWG" HANNER, *defensive tackle*
WILLIE DAVIS, *defensive end*
DAVE ROBINSON, *outside linebacker*
RAY NITSCHKE, *middle linebacker*
CLARKE HINKLE, *outside linebacker*
HERB ADDERLEY, *cornerback*
WILLIE WOOD, *free safety*
BOBBY DILLON, *strong safety*
WILLIE BUCHANON, *cornerback*
MAX McGEE, *punter*
RYAN LONGWELL, *kicker*
DESMOND HOWARD, *punt returner*
TRAVIS WILLIAMS, *kick returner*

VINCE LOMBARDI, *head coach*

DON HUTSON
End (1935–45)
Pro Bowls (4),* consensus All-Pro (5),
Hall of Fame (1963, charter member)

He was the best athlete I played with or against. He was a gifted receiver and a great defensive player. He could play in today's league and be a star. He had all the moves, the speed, the hands. He caught the ball in those years, and he could have caught them in any year.

Tony Canadeo
on Hutson

---

* *Postseason all-star games against the newly crowned league champion were played from 1938 to 1942, preceding the modern Pro Bowl, which began after the 1951 season. The National Football League recognizes those five all-star games as Pro Bowls.*

CAL HUBBARD
Tackle (1929–33, 1935)
consensus All-Pro (2),
Hall of Fame (1963, charter member)

The greatest tackle I've ever seen or been pulverized by.

Red Grange
on Hubbard

MIKE MICHALSKE
Guard (1929–35, 1937)
consensus All-Pro (2), Hall of Fame (1964)

Some might say Fuzzy or Gale from the modern era, but Michalske—"Iron Mike"—was the anvil of the great Packer line that helped gain Green Bay its first trio of NFL championships: Lambeau's three-peat contingent of 1929–31. Explosive quickness off the ball, stamina, and toughness marked Michalske's play, earning him a bust in Canton.

JIM RINGO
Center (1953–63)
Pro Bowls (7), consensus All-Pro (5),
Hall of Fame (1981)

Undersized but quick and intelligent, Ringo notched eight All-Pro honors and 10 Pro Bowl selections in his 15-year NFL career, 11 with the Packers, four with the Philadelphia Eagles. He anchored Lombardi's first two championship teams, in 1961 and '62, and once held the NFL record for most consecutive starts (183; 126 with Green Bay).

JERRY KRAMER
Guard (1958–68)
Pro Bowls (3), consensus All-Pro (2)

If you told Jerry Kramer to throw a block on a tractor-trailer, he'd give it a try.

Vince Lombardi

FORREST GREGG
Tackle (1956, 1958–70)
Pro Bowls (9), consensus All-Pro (4),
Hall of Fame (1977)

The finest football player I ever coached.

Vince Lombardi

STERLING SHARPE
Wide Receiver (1988–94)
Pro Bowls (5), consensus All-Pro (3)

Sharpe prematurely retired due to a career-threatening neck injury at the close of the 1994 season. He owns or shares six Packer receiving records.

I'm a big fan of Jerry Rice, and I coached him in San Francisco, but I'm not sure Sterling has to step back for anybody.

Mike Holmgren

BART STARR
Quarterback (1956–71)
Pro Bowls (4), consensus All-Pro (1),
NFL MVP (1966), Super Bowl MVP (1966, 1967),
Hall of Fame (1977)

Bart was rarely the best quarterback in the league on a statistical basis. But for three hours each Sunday, he was—almost always—the best quarterback in the game in which he was playing.

Jerry Kramer

JOHNNY BLOOD
Receiver/Halfback (1929–33, 1935–36)
consensus All-Pro (1),
Hall of Fame (1963, charter member)

Johnny "Blood" McNally, a halfback with speed and great hands, was the class of his day as a receiver coming out of the backfield. Were he playing today, he unquestionably would line up as a wide receiver.

The player who really made Lambeau's offense sing was Johnny Blood, the vagabond halfback from New Richmond, Wisconsin. Blood could do everything the rest of [his fellow backfield mates] could do, but he had one special talent they didn't have. Johnny Blood was one of the most dangerous pass receivers in the game of his day. He could slip out of the backfield, elude every defensive back that got in his way, then go up high between two defenders and come down with the ball. Once in the open field, it was a good bet he would score.

Larry Names

PAUL HORNUNG
Halfback (1957–62, 1964–66)
Pro Bowls (2), consensus All-Pro (1),
NFL MVP (1961), Hall of Fame (1986)

There's my offense.

Vince Lombardi

*after assessing game film
of Hornung soon after his
(Lombardi's) arrival in Green
Bay in 1959*

JIM TAYLOR
Fullback (1958–66)
Pro Bowls (5), consensus All-Pro (1),
NFL co-MVP (1962), Hall of Fame (1976)

I have never seen another football player with such balance, because he will stumble and stagger and still hold his feet. Where Jim Brown will give you that leg, then take it away from you, Jim Taylor will give it to you and ram it through your chest.

Vince Lombardi

REGGIE WHITE
Defensive End (1993–98)
Pro Bowls (6), consensus All-Pro (2)

Reggie White is the best defensive player in NFL history . . . the ultimate leader. The most amazing thing I've ever seen him do was throw the Dallas Cowboys' Larry Allen, a 330-pound [All-Pro] guard, to the turf like he was a rag doll. And that was in the game that Reggie had an elbow injury. He threw him five yards. Just tossed him in the air.

Brett Favre

HENRY JORDAN
Defensive Tackle (1959–69)
Pro Bowls (4), consensus All-Pro (2),
Hall of Fame (1995)

There's no question about him.

> **Green Bay coaching staff**
> *appraisal of Jordan after his*
> *rookie season*

———

DAVE "HAWG" HANNER
Defensive Tackle (1952–64)
Pro Bowls (2)

A popular Packer, Hanner's sturdy, smart play complemented the reckless abandon of fellow tackle Henry Jordan during the years (1959–64) the duo anchored the internal defensive wall of Lombardi's great teams. Hanner was a great pursuer on the field and a respected leader off it.

WILLIE DAVIS
Defensive End (1960–69)
Pro Bowls (5), consensus All-Pro (4),
Hall of Fame (1981)

A member of all five of the Lombardi era championship teams, Davis's durability is reflected by the fact that he never missed a game in his 10-year career as a Packer. Was equally proficient at stuffing the run or rushing the passer. Holds the Packer career record for most fumble recoveries (21).

DAVE ROBINSON
Outside Linebacker (1963–72)
Pro Bowls (2), consensus All-Pro (1)

Trying to throw a pass over Dave Robinson is like trying to pass over the Empire State Building.

> **Jack Christiansen**
> *Hall of Fame defensive back (Detroit Lions) and former San Francisco 49ers head coach*

RAY NITSCHKE
Middle Linebacker (1958–72)
Pro Bowls (1), consensus All-Pro (1),
NFL Championship Game MVP (1962),
Hall of Fame (1978),
NFL 75th Anniversary All-Time Team

You could never relax around Ray Nitschke on the practice field—he was liable to cold-cock you with that club of a forearm he wielded. Ray became Lombardi's hit man. He and Chicago's Dick Butkus became the most feared players in the NFL.

Domenic Gentile

CLARKE HINKLE
Linebacker (1932–41)
Pro Bowls (3), consensus All-Pro (2),
Hall of Fame (1964)

Better known as the powerhouse fullback of the Packers' 1930s decade, Hinkle was named to the NFL's All-Time Two-Way Team in 1994. His punishing play at linebacker was legendary, especially the titanic collisions between he and the Chicago Bears' Bronko Nagurski that shook the playing field, one of pro football history's great mano a mano confrontations.

HERB ADDERLEY
Cornerback (1961–69)
Pro Bowls (5), consensus All-Pro (2),
Hall of Fame (1980)

The stellar corner played in four of the first six Super Bowls (two with Green Bay, two with Dallas, winning three of the four). He tallied 39 thefts in his Packer career, after Lombardi grudgingly turned him over to Phil Bengtson on defense. Adderley holds the team record for most career touchdowns scored on interceptions (7).

———

WILLIE WOOD
Free Safety (1960–71)
Pro Bowls (8), consensus All-Pro (2),
Hall of Fame (1989)

Mike Ditka of the Bears has said that no one has ever tackled him harder than our little Willie.

Vince Lombardi
on Wood

BOBBY DILLON
Strong Safety (1952–59)
Pro Bowls (4), consensus All-Pro (3)

Of all the people I know who are not in the Hall, he deserves to be in.

Ray Nitschke

on Packers career interception leader Dillon, who compiled 52 picks in just eight seasons; 51 in seven. By contrast, Packers Hall of Famers Willie Wood and Herb Adderley totaled only 48 in 12 years and 39 in nine seasons respectively

Dillon's career average of 6.5 interceptions per season beats Hall of Famers Dick "Night Train" Lane, Jack Christiansen, Emlen Tunnell, and Mel Blount, as well as fellow Packers Adderley and Wood.

WILLIE BUCHANON
Cornerback (1972–78)
Pro Bowls (3)

Considered the finest cornerback to enter the NFL in a generation when he was chosen by Green Bay as their top pick in 1972, Buchanon started as a rookie and amassed 21 career interceptions in his seven seasons with the team. He is listed in Packer annals for his four-interception game against San Diego in 1978, tying him with Bobby Dillon for most picks in a single game. He suffered two broken legs during his Green Bay tenure, yet still went on to play four more years with San Diego.

MAX MCGEE
Punter (1954, 1957–67)
Pro Bowls (1)

Craig Hentrich had a higher average and a few more punts overall, and Don Chandler was that master practitioner of dual foot skills—the punt and the place-kick—but both players totaled just seven years with Green Bay. McGee, better known for his tour de force in Super Bowl I as a game-breaking pass catcher, logged a respectable 41.6 career punting average over 12 seasons, second highest in Packer history for punters with more than 250 punts.

RYAN LONGWELL
Kicker (1997–)

What do you do with a man who breaks the immortal Don Hutson's 57-year club scoring record, establishes a new team standard for most career field goals, co-owns the mark for the longest field goal in Packer history, and is the most accurate field-goal kicker in Green Bay history? You place him on your all-time team without reservation.

DESMOND HOWARD
Punt Returner (1996, 1999)

The flying feet of Desmond Howard staked the Packers to a 7–0 lead with the [1996 NFC Divisional Playoff] game just 2:15 old. Seven 49ers had a clear shot to tackle Howard on Tommy Thompson's first punt, but he made them all miss on a 71-yard touchdown return. It was Howard's fifth punt return for a score that year—one in the exhibition season, three in regular season, one in the postseason.

Bob McGinn
author

Howard culminated his superlative 1996 campaign by being named Super Bowl XXXI MVP, the first special teams player to ever gain the award.

TRAVIS WILLIAMS
Kick Returner (1967–70)

Others—Steve Odom, Al Carmichael, Herb Adderley, Dave Hampton—may have logged more career return yards, but no one in NFL history ever injected more abject fear into a kicking team than "the Roadrunner." Williams is the only Packer to score on a kickoff and punt return in the same game, but it is his single-season NFL-record 41.06-yard average per kick return, set during his rookie season, that still defies belief. His four kick returns for touchdowns in a single season (1967) is another NFL mark that still stands.

VINCE LOMBARDI
Head Coach (1959–67)
Hall of Fame (1971)

The toughest all-time team decision by far. How do you possibly pick against either Lombardi or Curly Lambeau? Without Lambeau, there are no Green Bay Packers. Yet no coach in NFL history ever equaled Lombardi's five championships in seven years. I let the players decide it. A quote earlier in this book that referenced opinions by Cal Hubbard, Mike Michalske, Johnny Blood, and Clarke Hinkle on the quality of Lambeau's coaching stuck in my head: All claimed Lambeau was not much of a strategist. Those comments, coming from the caliber of those Hall of Famers, swung it in Vince's favor. Lombardi was the ultimate architect, the unsurpassed master of strategy and planning—not to mention his immortal status as a motivator.

NFL MVPs

1941	DON HUTSON
1942	DON HUTSON
1961	PAUL HORNUNG
1962	JIM TAYLOR
	(co-MVP with Y. A. Tittle)
1966	BART STARR
1995	BRETT FAVRE
1996	BRETT FAVRE
1997	BRETT FAVRE
	(co-MVP with Barry Sanders)

RETIRED PACKER NUMBERS

3 TONY CANADEO, halfback (1941–44, 1946–52)
jersey retired: 1952

14 DON HUTSON, end (1935–45)
jersey retired: 1951

15 BART STARR, quarterback (1956–71)
jersey retired: 1973

66 RAY NITSCHKE, middle linebacker (1958–72)
jersey retired: 1983

NFL ROOKIES OF THE YEAR

1959 BOYD DOWLER
(co-Rookie of the Year with Nick Pietrosante)

1971 JOHN BROCKINGTON

FIELDS OF PLAY

John Madden said that if there is such a thing as a shrine to pro football, Lambeau Field is it.

Brett Favre

From 1919 through 1922, the Packers played home games in Hagemeister Park in Green Bay. When the park was dug up in 1923 to build a new East High School, the Packers moved to Bellevue Park for the 1923 and '24 seasons.

Don Davenport

In 1925, the Packers moved into City Stadium built on the grounds of East High School along the East River. The initial grandstand seating capacity was 6,000 with additional space beyond the end zones for standing room only customers.

Larry Names

There was a great deal of tradition wound up in the old stadium on the East Side. It was practically the birthplace of the team back in 1919.

John B. Torinus

The old wooden stands at City Stadium were inadequate and there were practically no modern facilities at the stadium. Both the Packers and the visiting teams dressed in the locker room at East High School. Early on the teams would gather in a circle at opposite ends of the field for their half-time rest and regrouping talks.

John B. Torinus

The locker room was horrendous. It was underneath the stands. There were concrete floors. It was from the medieval ages.

John Martinkovic
defensive end (1951–56),
on the old City Stadium

The Packers played their first home game in Milwaukee in 1933, at State Fair Park. They lost to the New York Giants, 10–7.

Don Davenport

County Stadium was a baseball field with both benches on the same sideline. And even though seating and many other amenities didn't compare to Lambeau, the Packers enjoyed a lot of success at the former home of the Braves and the Brewers, finishing with a 105–61–3 mark [.630].

Todd Mishler

author, on the Packers "other" home, in Milwaukee (1953–94)

It [Milwaukee] was the site for Green Bay's first NFL championship won on Wisconsin soil, in 1939, and the team also claimed the 1967 Western Conference title there.

Todd Mishler

on Milwaukee's State Fair Park and County Stadium

Sitting in the tape room, icing down, there was a kind of melancholy. It was the last time I would be taped up here, the last time I would shower here, the last time I would play here. It has been a nice 10 years of coming down here to the Milwaukee fans.

Ken Ruettgers

*offensive tackle (1985–96),
on the last Packers game played
at County Stadium, a 21–17
victory over Atlanta, Dec. 18,
1994*

It is kind of sad to end something that has been really good to us. I don't think a lot of the players feel the way I do about the change. It definitely hit me. It's an emotional thing for me. I appreciate the fans here and all the cheers and handshakes that I've gotten from the people of Milwaukee.

> **Ed West**
> *tight end (1984–94),*
> *on the Pack's last game at*
> *County Stadium*

The present Packers' stadium opened on Sept. 29, 1957, and was originally named New City Stadium. Not until 1965, after the death of Packers co-founder Curly Lambeau, was it renamed Lambeau Field.

Don Davenport

The new City Stadium was finally completed in time for the opening of the 1957 season. . . . A parade, consisting of six marching sections, variety acts, and interspersed with 35 floats, began at Ashland Avenue and West Walnut and proceeded to old City Stadium where television actor James Arness, who portrayed Marshal Matt Dillon in the TV series *Gunsmoke*, and Miss America, Marilyn Van Derbur, were entertaining the crowd waiting there.

Larry Names

Then-Vice President Richard M. Nixon also spoke at the dedication ceremonies.

The Packers have played in several different homes over the years. They've played on fields marked off in local parks, fields without fences to control crowds, baseball stadia, and one of the finest football arenas in the history of the game: Lambeau Field.

Larry Names

Nostalgia and mystique still reign at the venerable site, and Packer players and their foes are reminded by the large gold letters that display names of the 19 Green Bay greats in the NFL Hall of Fame and the numerals for the years that represent the team's record 12 championship seasons.

Todd Mishler
on Lambeau Field

In 1998, *Sports Illustrated* named Lambeau Field the No. 8 venue in the world to watch sports, with no other NFL stadium making the magazine's top 20 list.

Todd Mishler

I loved Lambeau Field. It was my favorite place to play. Playing on the grass was one reason, and the intimacy of the stadium was another. The fans were so close to the field, and they knew their football. After the game, in the parking lot, they'd feed you bratwurst, steak, a beer or two. We got invited into people's trailers, even after beating them a couple of times.

Darrin Nelson
Minnesota Vikings running back
(1982–89, 1991–92)

Being at Lambeau was a big deal, the mystique of playing there and being around that atmosphere. The first time out of the locker room there I couldn't fathom what it was like. They had something going on that I didn't know anything about. The Cheeseheads, they were a thorn in our side.

Carl Lee
Minnesota Vikings cornerback
(1983–93)

Packer fans have been tailgating from Day One. I can remember going to games and it's freezing outside and these people are half-naked at 10 a.m. for a 1 p.m. kickoff. I was totally amazed to see that kind of support in a small town.

Dale Hackbart
defensive back (1960–61)

I just love the history of it. I love the small community. It reminds me of when I was going to play my high school games on Friday night. You turn the corner, and there the stadium is. You walk out the same tunnel the Cowboys walked out of in the Ice Bowl. Everything is exactly the same, for the most part, given a few upgrades. But the history, and Lombardi, and the fans, and playing against a great team and a great franchise like the Packers, that's why it's my favorite.

Cris Carter
*former Minnesota Vikings/
Miami Dolphins wide receiver,
on Lambeau Field*

Whenever we play at home, I try to watch the visiting team when they get to the stadium. . . . You can see them staring. These are players now, not fans. They look up at the names of all the great Packer Hall of Famers and then they look at all the championship seasons, all those numbers painted at the top of the stadium. Everytime I see that, it reminds me of what an incredibly special place this is.

Bob Harlan

RIVALRIES

As far as tradition, history, and rivalry, this is THE football game.

> **Paul Tagliabue**
> *NFL commissioner,*
> *at Lambeau Field for the*
> *150th meeting of the Packers*
> *and Bears, Nov. 12, 1995*

The shrewd Mr. Halas and his big bad Bears always will stand out as the Green Bay Packers' oldest and bitterest foes. Throughout the rivalry dating back to their first meeting in 1921, they have established one of modern football's leading Hatfield-McCoy feuds.

Arch Ward
1945

In a time of domed stadiums and artificial turf, the Packers and the Bears still play football in its most basic form: outside, on real grass, in rain, sleet, hail, or snow.

Glenn Swain
author

When Packer fans think of Chicago, their blood pressure rises.

Larry Names

After more than 70 years of football, the average score of a game between the Packers and Bears is Bears 17, Packers 15. It's that close.

Glenn Swain

(The above calculation is from the years 1921–1995.)

Already in 1933, the newspapers were making a big deal out of how the Packers and Bears had the longest playing tradition in the NFL. Over those years, they had played 26 contests, with the Packers winning 12, the Bears winning 10, and there were four ties.

Larry Names

The Packers swept the Chicago Bears in 1935, winning 7–0 on Sept. 22 and 17–14 on Oct. 27. It would be 26 years before a Green Bay team would complete another sweep of the Bears—in 1961, when the Pack prevailed 24–0 and 31–28.

Don Davenport

If Lambeau caught you even smiling during "Bear Week," you were in trouble.

Tony Canadeo

The first time I carried the ball against the Bears, I went off tackle and came up spitting teeth!

Tony Canadeo

It was the hardest hit I've ever seen.

Gary Knafelc

on Bears linebacker George Connor's near-annihilation of Veryl Switzer on a kick return, Nov. 6, 1955. WGN broadcaster Jack Brickhouse said the hit could be heard all over Wrigley Field

I went up into the air, my helmet went off my head with the strap still intact, and I didn't know what had happened. . . . He basically destroyed me on that play.

Veryl Switzer

halfback/kick returner (1954–55)

The Packers' blocking wedge evaporated before the oncoming charge of the Bears' Connor, a future Hall of Famer, suddenly exposing Switzer to a straight-on, unavoidably vicious hit. Switzer's sternum was torn loose on the play.

I never saw him and he never saw me. It was just two people at the wrong place at the wrong time.

George Connor
*Chicago Bears Hall of Fame
tackle/linebacker (1948–55),
on his devastating hit of Packers
kick returner Veryl Switzer*

The Packers' games were probably more physical than most other games because they were such a rival. You read the papers all week long and the coaches are all talking about this player and that player, and it gets intense. Both teams would then leave everything out on the field.

Harlon Hill

I'm from Chicago and I always dreamed of playing at Wrigley Field. Then when I finally did, people screamed things and threw garbage at me. But there's nothing like the Packers against the Bears.

Ray Nitschke

We called it "Packers Panic Week." Guys were just totally different in attitude going into that game. That's when I learned it wasn't just another game. It was take-no-prisoners, whoever is left standing, wins. It was two old warriors going at it. After it's said and done with, you respect each other.

Doug Buffone
Chicago Bears linebacker (1966–79), who played in 38 Packers-Bears contests, including preseason games

It was nothing to be staying at the old Northland Hotel and at 3 o'clock in the morning hear someone playing "Bear Down Chicago Bears" with a trombone. Or someone pulls the fire alarm at 4 a.m. and players in their shorts start running out the door, then stand there in front of a bunch of Packers' fans wearing antlers on their heads.

Doug Buffone

It's tough to get your butt kicked on national TV. It's embarrassing. It stinks.

Joe Cain
*Chicago Bears linebacker
(1993–96), after Green Bay's
33–6 decimation of the Bears
on Halloween night 1994 at
Soldier Field*

It was also throwbacks uniform night. The Packers wore white travel jerseys with gold topping around the shoulder pads, khaki-colored pants, and dull yellow helmets without any insignia.

It was a toe-to-toe, blow-by-blow kind of game.

Ken Ruettgers
on Green Bay's 27–24 win at
Soldier Field, Sept. 11, 1995—
the Pack's eighth straight victory
over the Bears on Monday
Night Football

I don't think anything can make me feel good. Not after losing to Green Bay.

Jim Flanigan
Chicago Bears defensive tackle
(1994–2000)

It used to be the Packers and Bears because Mike Ditka was in Chicago and Forrest Gregg was here, but this [Minnesota-Green Bay rivalry] has taken over.

Larry Primeau

*Packer fan known as
"the Packelope," for his vintage
Green Bay helmet mounted with
10-point buck antlers*

Anytime you get into one of these rivalry games, you're going to have unusual plays like that. And usually those unusual plays affect the outcome of the game.

Dennis Green

*former Minnesota Vikings head
coach, on the "Immaculate
Deflection," Antonio Freeman's
miraculous catch and run of
Minnesota cornerback Cris
Dishman's twice-tipped ball for
the Packers' game-winning touchdown, on* Monday Night
Football, *Nov. 6, 2000*

I saw it on the field, and I couldn't believe he caught it. It's one of those things that can happen but is still hard to believe.

Ahman Green
running back (2000–),
on Antonio Freeman's
Immaculate Deflection

Cris Carter, it was so irritating to watch him whine about wanting to get every call against our DBs, and that's what added to the rivalry for me.

Larry Primeau
on the Green Bay-Minnesota
rivalry

Three or four times I remember we played at the end of the year either at Lambeau or Metropolitan Stadium. Much of the time the field was frozen. As tough as it was on the players, it was even tougher for the fans that came out all bundled up. But that's the way the Packers and Vikings should do battle.

Stu Voigt
Minnesota Vikings tight end
(1970–80)

It seemed like we always played the Vikings the first week of deer season. You never wanted to get hurt because then you'd have to spend Monday in the training room instead of going hunting. Jerry Kramer would take a carload of us to some place up by Rhinelander.

Dave Robinson

If there's one team in the National Football League I'd like to embarrass, it would be the Dallas Cowboys.

Brett Favre

who, in eight attempts, has never won at Texas Stadium (through 2003)

We went into Texas Stadium and let the game slip away. We let them take control. We played them as tough as we could, but late in the game we just didn't believe we could win.

Brett Favre

on the bitter 38–27 NFC Championship Game loss to Dallas in 1995

We want the ball, and we're going to score.

Matt Hasselbeck

*Seattle Seahawks quarterback, to
referee Bernie Kukar at the
midfield coin toss before the start
of sudden-death overtime in the
2003 Wild Card Playoff Game,
on Jan. 4, 2004, eventually won
by Green Bay on cornerback
Al Harris's interception return
of a Hasselbeck pass for the
game-winning touchdown*

THE LOCKER ROOM

He has healing powers beyond all of us. It's really true. The guy is a freak of nature in regards to his body.

Mike Sherman

head coach (2000–), on Brett Favre after the 2003 season. It was determined that Favre, who played with a broken thumb on his passing hand for 11 games that season and extended his consecutive starting streak to 208 games, would not require off-season surgery

Two weeks ago, I didn't believe in that [divine providence], but now . . . something is going on here.

Brett Favre

on the miraculous close of the 2003 regular season, in which the Packers steamrollered Denver, 31–3, on the final Sunday, while the Arizona Cardinals knocked NFC North rival Minnesota out of the division title picture and the playoffs with their improbable 18–17 come-from-behind victory on the last play of the game, elevating the Packers to the division championship. Adding to the miracle was Favre's other-worldly performance on Monday Night Football *the previous week—a first-half, four-touchdown-pass explosion over Oakland the day after his father, Irvin, died of a heart attack*

If you don't win, people don't notice you; I don't care how good you are.

Brett Favre

We got rid of the only two coaches the Packers ever had. Bob Forte and I were the only ones left from Lambeau's teams. We were the only guys who played for the only two coaches the Packers ever had.

Dick Wildung
two-way tackle (1946–51, 1953), who played at the end of the Curly Lambeau era and through the Gene Ronzani years (1950–53), part of an 11-year era signifying the worst years in Green Bay history

In 1980, the Chicago Bears' Vince Evans became the only player to fashion a perfect 158.3 passer rating in a game against the Packers [minimum 20 attempts].

Eric Goska
author

According to the organization's by-laws, if for some strange reason the Packers had to be sold, the money would go to Green Bay's Sullivan-Wallen American Legion Post. Let's see, the Packers are valued at about $170 million or so. Man, those Legionnaires could have one helluva party with that bundle.

Brett Favre

This arrangement existed from 1923 until a stockholder vote in the late 1990s, when the beneficiary was changed to the Packers Foundation.

When the team was on the road, the wives would get together and play bridge and rehearse little songs we would sing when they got home. We listened to the games on radio. When we went to Milwaukee for a game, even there Curly [Lambeau] was so darn strict. We weren't allowed to be anywhere near the same train car they [the players] were in. We had to be way back in the caboose. We stayed at the same hotel, but not in the same room! They were very strict about that, but we could go to church together.

Ruth Canadeo
Tony Canadeo's wife

Everybody asks the question, Would you do it again? Everyone always dreams about playing in the NFL. I've just had my 17th surgery on my right knee. You're heroes while you're there, but you see the old guys going through what they go through. I'm 41 years old, and in another six months I'm going to have a knee replacement. I mean, boy, it's a price. While you're doing it, you don't think about it, because you have that sense of invincibility. But when you get to be 40, when you start looking back on it, you think, *What did I do!*

Brian Noble
linebacker (1985–93)

If you talk to any player who has retired, they'll tell you the thing they miss most is hanging out with the guys. I guarantee it's not the practices.

Brett Favre

People just don't talk about the 1940s and '50s. It's like they don't exist. People don't write about it or talk about it. It's the '30s or the '60s."

Floyd "Breezy" Reid
halfback (1950–56), on the Packers' "Dark Ages." During the 11-year span, 1948–58, Green Bay went 37–93–2 and failed to produce one team with a winning record

In 1964, Paul Hornung missed more field goals in a single season [26], than any other player in NFL history.

Eric Goska

There aren't any seats left; the place is filled to captivity.

> **George Whitney Calhoun**
> Green Bay Press-Gazette
> *editor and Packer promoter*
> *through the team's first 28 years.*
> *"Cal" was renowned for his use*
> *of malaprops. Among other lines*
> *attributed to him: "Like looking*
> *for a weasel in a haystack" and*
> *"Now he'll have to pedal his*
> *own canoe"*

In 1942, Cecil Isbell, needed fewer completions [10] than any other passer in team history to reach the 300-yard mark in a single game.

> **Eric Goska**

For God so loved the Packers He sent Reggie.

> **Sign outside First United**
> **Church of Christ**
> *in Green Bay the morning of*
> *Super Bowl XXXI*

PACKERS WORLD CHAMPIONSHIP ROSTERS

No team has recorded more NFL championships than The Little Town That Could. Green Bay's 12 world crowns place it in the rarified company of a handful of elite major sports franchises. Only baseball's New York Yankees (26), hockey's Montreal Canadiens (24), and the NBA's Boston Celtics (16) claim more world championships.

1929

12–0–1

Earl "Curly" Lambeau, head coach

	Pos	Ht	Wt	College
Ashmore, Roger	T	6–1	212	Gonzaga
Baker, Roy "Bullet"	BB	6–0	177	USC
Bowdoin, James	G	6–2	220	Alabama
Cahoon, Ivan	T	6–2	235	Gonzaga
Darling, Bernard "Boob"	C	6–1	206	Beloit
Dilweg, LaVern "Lavvie"	E	6–3	200	Marquette
Dunn, Joseph "Red"	QB	6–0	178	Marquette
Earp, Francis "Jug"	T	6–1	235	Monmouth
Evans, Jack	BB	6–0	195	California
Hill, Don	WB	5–11	190	Stanford
Hubbard, Robert "Cal"	T	6–5	250	Geneva
Kern, William	T	6–0	187	Pittsburgh
Kotal, Eddie	HB	5–10	165	Lawrence
Lambeau, Earl "Curly"	TB	6–0	190	Notre Dame
Lewellen, Verne	HB	6–2	181	Nebraska
Lidberg, Carl "Cully"	FB	6–0	200	Minnesota
McCrary, Herdis	FB	6–2	205	Georgia
McNally, Johnny "Blood"	HB	6–1	188	St. John's
Michalske, August "Mike"	G	6–0	210	Penn State
Minick, Paul	G	6–0	195	Iowa
Molenda, John "Bo"	FB	5–10	210	Michigan
Nash, Tom	E	6–3	208	Georgia
O'Donnell, Dick	E	6–0	190	Minnesota
Perry, Claude "Cupid"	T	6–1	210	Alabama
Smith, Richard "Red"	BB	5–10	192	Notre Dame
Woodin, Howard "Whitey"	G	5–10	208	Marquette
Young, Billy	G	5–10	210	Ohio State
Zuidmulder, Dave	TB	5–10	175	Georgetown

1930

10–3–1

Earl "Curly" Lambeau, head coach

	Pos	Ht	Wt	College
Bloodgood, Elbert "Al"	T	5–8	153	Nebraska
Bowdoin, James	G	6–2	220	Alabama
Darling, Bernard "Boob"	C	6–1	206	Beloit
Dilweg, LaVern "Lavvie"	E	6–3	200	Marquette
Dunn, Joseph "Red"	QB	6–0	178	Marquette
Earp, Francis "Jug"	T	6–1	235	Monmouth
Engelmann, Wuert	HB	6–3	191	South Dakota St.
Fitzgibbon, Paul	BB	5–8	176	Creighton
Franta, Herb "Chief"	T	6–1	220	St. Thomas "MN"
Hanny, Frank "Duke"	E	6–0	199	Indiana
Haycraft, Ken	E	6–0	178	Minnesota
Herber, Arnie	TB	5–11	203	Regis
Hubbard, Robert "Cal"	T	6–5	250	Geneva
Kern, William	T	6–0	187	Pittsburgh
Lewellen, Verne	HB	6–2	181	Nebraska
Lidberg, Carl "Cully"	FB	6–0	200	Minnesota
McCrary, Herdis	FB	6–2	205	Georgia
McNally, Johnny "Blood"	HB	6–1	188	St. John's
Michalske, August "Mike"	G	6–0	210	Penn State
Molenda. John "Bo"	FB	5–10	210	Michigan
Nash, Tom	E	6–3	208	Georgia
O'Donnell, Dick	E	6–0	190	Minnesota
Pape, Oran "Nanny"	TB	5–11	180	Iowa
Perry, Claude "Cupid"	T	6–1	210	Alabama
Radick, Ken	E	5–10	210	Marquette
Sleight, Elmer "Red"	T	6–2	226	Purdue
Woodin, Howard "Whitey"	G	5–10	208	Marquette
Zuidmulder, Dave	TB	5–10	175	Georgetown
Zuver, Merle	G	6–1	198	Nebraska

1931
12–2
Earl "Curly" Lambeau, head coach

	Pos	Ht	Wt	College
Baker, Frank	E	6–2	182	Northwestern
Barrager, Nate	C	6–0	212	USC
Bowdoin, James	G	6–2	220	Alabama
Bruder, Hank	BB	6–0	199	Northwestern
Comstock, Rudy	G	5–10	209	Georgetown
Darling, Bernard "Boob"	C	6–1	206	Beloit
Davenport, Wayne "Mike"	HB	6–4	187	Hardin-Simmons
Dilweg, LaVern "Lavvie"	E	6–3	200	Marquette
Don Carlos, Waldo	C	6–2	190	Drake
Dunn, Joseph "Red"	QB	6–0	178	Marquette
Earp, Francis "Jug"	T	6–1	235	Monmouth
Engelmann, Wuert	HB	6–3	191	South Dakota St.
Fitzgibbon, Paul	BB	5–8	176	Creighton
Gantenbein, Milt	E	6–0	199	Wisconsin
Grove, Roger "Roy"	BB	6–0	182	Michigan State
Herber, Arnie	TB	5–11	203	Regis
Hubbard, Robert "Cal"	T	6–5	250	Geneva
Jenison, Ray	T	6–2	224	South Dakota St.
Johnston, Chester "Swede"	FB	5–8	196	Marquette
Lewellen, Verne	HB	6–2	181	Nebraska
McCrary, Herdis	FB	6–2	205	Georgia
McNally, Johnny "Blood"	HB	6–1	188	St. John's
Michalske, August "Mike"	G	6–0	210	Penn State
Molenda. John "Bo"	FB	5–10	210	Michigan
Nash, Tom	E	6–3	208	Georgia
Perry, Claude "Cupid"	T	6–1	210	Alabama
Radick, Ken	E	5–10	210	Marquette
Saunders, Russ "Racehorse"	FB	5–9	190	USC
Sleight, Elmer "Red"	T	6–2	226	Purdue
Stahlman, Dick	T	6–2	219	Northwestern
Wilson, Faye "Mule"	WB	5–11	192	Texas A&M
Woodin, Howard "Whitey"	G	5–10	208	Marquette
Zuidmulder, Dave	TB	5–10	175	Georgetown

1936
11–1–1 (includes 21–6 NFL Championship Game win over Boston)
Earl "Curly" Lambeau, head coach

	Pos	Ht	Wt	College
Becker, Wayland	E	6–0	198	Marquette
Bruder, Hank	BB	6–0	199	Northwestern
Butler, Frank	C	6–3	237	Michigan State
Clemens, Cal	BB	6–1	195	USC
Engebretsen, Paul "Tiny"	G	6–1	238	Northwestern
Evans, Lon	G	6–2	223	TCU
Gantenbein, Milt	E	6–0	199	Wisconsin
Goldenberg, Charles "Buckets"	G	5–10	220	Wisconsin
Gordon, Lou	T	6–5	224	Illinois
Herber, Arnie	TB	5–11	203	Regis
Hinkle, Clarke	FB	5–11	202	Bucknell
Hutson, Don	E	6–1	183	Alabama
Johnston, Chester "Swede"	FB	5–8	196	Marquette
Kiesling, Walt "Babe"	G	6–2	249	St. Thomas
Laws, Joe	HB	5–9	186	Iowa
Letlow, Russ	G	6–0	214	San Francisco
Mattos, Harry	TB	6–0	198	St. Mary's
McNally, Johnny "Blood"	HB	6–1	188	St. John's
Miller, Paul	HB	5–11	180	South Dakota St.
Monnett, Bob	TB	5–9	182	Michigan State
Paulekas, Tony	G	5–10	210	Wash. & Jefferson
Rose, Al "Big Un"	E	6–3	205	Texas
Sauer, George	HB	6–2	208	Nebraska
Scherer, Bernie	E	6–1	190	Nebraska
Schneidman, Herm	BB	5–11	201	Iowa
Schwammel, Ade	T	6–2	225	Oregon State
Seibold, Champ	T	6–4	237	Wisconsin
Smith, Ernie	T	6–2	224	USC
Svendsen, George	C	6–4	230	Minnesota

1939
10—2 (includes 27—0 NFL Championship Game win over New York)
Earl "Curly" Lambeau, head coach

	Pos	Ht	Wt	College
Balasz, Frank	FB	6—2	212	Iowa
Biolo, John	G	5—10	191	Lake Forest
Brennan, Jack	G	6—1	204	Michigan
Brock, Charley "Ears"	C	6—2	207	Nebraska
Bruder, Hank	BB	6—0	199	Northwestern
Buhler, Larry	FB	6—2	210	Minnesota
Craig, Larry "Superman"	BB	6—1	211	South Carolina
Engebretsen, Paul "Tiny"	G	6—1	238	Northwestern
Gantenbein, Milt	E	6—0	199	Wisconsin
Goldenberg, Charles "Buckets"	G	5—10	220	Wisconsin
Greenfield, Tom	C	6—4	213	Arizona
Herber, Arnie	TB	5—11	203	Regis
Hinkle, Clarke	FB	5—11	202	Bucknell
Hutson, Don	E	6—1	183	Alabama
Isbell, Cecil	TB	6—1	190	Purdue
Jacunski, Harry	E	6—2	200	Fordham
Jankowski, Ed	FB	5—9	201	Wisconsin
Kell, Paul	T	6—2	217	Notre Dame
Kilbourne, Wally "Cleats"	T	6—3	240	Minnesota
Lawrence, Jimmy	WB	5—11	190	TCU
Laws, Joe	HB	5—9	186	Iowa
Lee, Bill	T	6—2	231	Alabama
Letlow, Russ	G	6—0	214	San Francisco
Moore, Al	DE	6—2	218	Texas A&M
Mulleneaux, Carl "Moose"	DE	6—3	209	Utah State
Ray, Buford "Baby"	T	6—6	249	Vanderbilt
Schneidman, Herm	BB	5—11	201	Iowa
Schultz, Charlie	T	6—3	231	Minnesota
Smith, Ernie	T	6—2	224	USC
Steen, Frank	E	6—1	190	Rice
Svendsen, Bud	C	6—1	190	Minnesota
Thompson, Tuffy	HB	5—11	172	Minnesota
Tinsley, Pete	G	5—8	205	Georgia
Twedell, Frank	G	5—11	220	Minnesota
Uram, Andy	HB	5—10	188	Minnesota
Weisgerber, Dick	BB	5—10	200	Willamette
Zarnas, Gust	G	5—10	220	Ohio State
Zoll, Dick	G	5—11	218	Indiana

1944
9–2 (includes 14–7 NFL Championship Game win over New York)
Earl "Curly" Lambeau, head coach

	Pos	Ht	Wt	College
Berezney, Paul	T	6–2	221	Fordham
Bilda, Dick	TB	6–2	210	Marquette
Brock, Charley "Ears"	C	6–2	207	Nebraska
Brock, Lou	HB	6–0	195	Purdue
Bucchianeri, Mike	G	5–10	212	Indiana
Canadeo, Tony	HB	5–11	190	Gonzaga
Comp, Irv	TB	6–2	204	Benedictine
Craig, Larry "Superman"	BB	6–1	211	South Carolina
Croft, Milburn "Tiny"	T	6–3	287	Ripon
Duhart, Paul	HB	6–0	180	Florida
Flowers, Bob	C	6–1	210	Texas Tech
Fritsch, Ted	FB/LB	5–10	210	Wis.-Stevens Pt.
Goldenberg, Charles "Buckets"	G	5–10	220	Wisconsin
Hutson, Don	E	6–1	183	Alabama
Jacunski, Harry	E	6–2	200	Fordham
Kahler, Bob	HB	6–3	201	Nebraska
Kercher, Bob	DE	6–2	196	Georgetown
Kuusisto, Bill	G	6–0	228	Minnesota
Laws, Joe	HB	5–9	186	Iowa
Mason, Joel	E	6–0	199	W. Michigan
McKay, Roy "Tex"	TB	6–0	193	Texas
McPherson, Forrest	C	5–11	233	Nebraska
Perkins, Don "Butch"	FB	6–0	196	Wis.-Platteville
Ray, Buford "Baby"	T	6–6	249	Vanderbilt
Schwammel, Ade	T	6–2	225	Oregon State
Sorenson, Glen "Goof"	G	6–0	217	Utah State
Starret, Ben	BB	5–11	213	St. Mary's
Tinsley, Pete	G	5–8	205	Georgia
Tollefson, Chuck	G	6–0	215	Iowa
Urban, Alex "Jeep"	DE	6–3	207	South Carolina
Wehba, Ray	E	6–0	215	USC

1961

12–3 (includes 37–0 NFL Championship Game win over New York Giants)
Vince Lombardi, head coach

	Pos	Ht	Wt	College
Adderley, Herb	CB	6–0	205	Michigan State
Agajanian, "Bootin'" Ben	K	6–0	215	New Mexico
Bettis, Tom	LB	6–2	228	Purdue
Carpenter, Lew	FB	6–1	220	Arkansas
Currie, Dan	LB	6–3	235	Michigan State
Davidson, Ben	DE	6–8	275	East L.A. J.C.
Davis, Willie	DE	6–3	243	Grambling St.
Dowler, Boyd	E	6–5	224	Colorado
Folkins, Lee	DE	6–5	215	Washington
Forester, Bill	LB	6–3	237	SMU
Gregg, Forrest	T	6–4	249	SMU
Gremminger, Hank	DB	6–1	201	Baylor
Hanner, Dave (Hawg)	DT	6–2	257	Arkansas
Hornung, Paul	HB	6–2	215	Notre Dame
Iman, Ken	C	6–1	240	S.E. Missouri St.
Jordan, Henry	DT	6–2	248	Virginia
Knafelc, Gary	E	6–4	217	Colorado
Kostelnik, Ron	DT	6–4	260	Cincinnati
Kramer, Jerry	G	6–3	245	Idaho
Kramer, Ron	E	6–3	234	Michigan
Masters, Norm	T	6–2	249	Michigan State
McGee, Max	E	6–3	205	Tulane
Moore, Tom	HB	6–2	215	Vanderbilt
Nitschke, Ray	LB	6–3	235	Illinois
Pitts, Elijah	HB	6–1	210	Philander Smith
Quinlan, Bill	DE	6–3	248	Michigan State
Ringo, Jim	C	6–1	232	Syracuse
Roach, John	QB	6–4	197	SMU
Skoronski, Bob	T	6–3	249	Indiana
Starr, Bart	QB	6–1	197	Alabama
Symank, John	DB	5–11	180	Florida
Taylor, Jim	FB	6–0	214	LSU
Thurston, Fuzzy	G	6–1	247	Valparaiso
Toburen, Nelson	LB	6–3	235	Wichita State
Tunnell, Emlen	DB	6–1	187	Iowa
Whittenton, Jesse	DB	6–0	193	Texas-El Paso
Wood, Willie	DB	5–10	190	USC

Starting lineups in bold

1962

14—1 (includes 16—7 NFL Championship Game win over New York Giants)
Vince Lombardi, head coach

	Pos	Ht	Wt	College
Adderley, Herb	CB	6—0	205	Michigan State
Barnes, Gary	E	6—4	200	Clemson
Blaine, Ed	G	6—1	240	Missouri
Carpenter, Lew	FB	6—1	220	Arkansas
Currie, Dan	LB	6—3	235	Michigan State
Davis, Willie	DE	6—3	243	Grambling St.
Dowler, Boyd	E	6—5	224	Colorado
Forester, Bill	LB	6—3	237	SMU
Gassert, Ron	DT	6—3	260	Virginia
Gregg, Forrest	T	6—4	249	SMU
Gremminger, Hank	DB	6—1	201	Baylor
Gros, Earl	FB	6—3	220	LSU
Hanner, Dave (Hawg)	DT	6—2	257	Arkansas
Hornung, Paul	HB	6—2	215	Notre Dame
Iman, Ken	C	6—1	240	S.E. Missouri St.
Jordan, Henry	DT	6—2	248	Virginia
Knafelc, Gary	E	6—4	217	Colorado
Kostelnik, Ron	DT	6—4	260	Cincinnati
Kramer, Jerry	G	6—3	245	Idaho
Kramer, Ron	E	6—3	234	Michigan
Masters, Norm	T	6—2	249	Michigan State
McGee, Max	E	6—3	205	Tulane
Moore, Tom	HB	6—2	215	Vanderbilt
Nitschke, Ray	LB	6—3	235	Illinois
Pitts, Elijah	HB	6—1	210	Philander Smith
Quinlan, Bill	DE	6—3	248	Michigan State
Ringo, Jim	C	6—1	232	Syracuse
Roach, John	QB	6—4	197	SMU
Skoronski, Bob	T	6—3	249	Indiana
Starr, Bart	QB	6—1	197	Alabama
Symank, John	DB	5—11	180	Florida
Taylor, Jim	FB	6—0	214	LSU
Thurston, Fuzzy	G	6—1	247	Valparaiso
Toburen, Nelson	LB	6—3	235	Wichita State
Whittenton, Jesse	DB	6—0	193	Texas-El Paso
Williams, Howie	DB	6—1	190	Howard
Wood, Willie	DB	5—10	190	USC

1965

12–3–1 (includes 23–12 NFL Championship Game win over Cleveland)
Vince Lombardi, head coach

	Pos	Ht	Wt	College
Adderley, Herb	CB	6–0	205	Michigan State
Aldridge, Lionel	DE	6–3	254	Utah State
Anderson, Bill	TE	6–3	211	Tennessee
Bowman, Ken	C	6–3	230	Wisconsin
Bratkowski, Zeke	QB	6–2	210	Georgia
Brown, Tom	DB	6–1	192	Maryland
Caffey, Lee Roy	LB	6–4	240	Texas A&M
Chandler, Don	K	6–2	215	Florida
Claridge, Dennis	QB	6–2	220	Nebraska
Coffey, Junior	HB	6–2	215	Washington
Crutcher, Tommy	LB	6–4	230	TCU
Curry, Bill	C	6–3	235	Georgia Tech
Dale, Carroll	WR	6–2	200	Virginia Tech
Davis, Willie	DE	6–3	243	Grambling St.
Dowler, Boyd	WR	6–5	224	Colorado
Fleming, Marv	TE	6–4	232	Utah
Gregg, Forrest	T	6–4	249	SMU
Gremminger, Hank	DB	6–1	201	Baylor
Grimm, Dan	G	6–3	245	Colorado
Hart, Doug	DB	6–0	190	Texas-Arlington
Hornung, Paul	HB	6–2	215	Notre Dame
Jacobs, Allen	HB	6–1	215	Utah
Jeter, Bob	DB	6–1	200	Iowa
Jordan, Henry	DT	6–2	248	Virginia
Kostelnik, Ron	DT	6–4	260	Cincinnati
Kramer, Jerry	G	6–3	245	Idaho
Long, Bob	WR	6–3	205	Wichita State
Marshall, Bud	DT	6–4	270	Stephen F. Austin
McGee, Max	E	6–3	205	Tulane
Moore, Tom	HB	6–2	215	Vanderbilt
Nitschke, Ray	LB	6–3	235	Illinois
Pitts, Elijah	HB	6–1	210	Philander Smith
Robinson, Dave	LB	6–3	245	Penn State
Skoronski, Bob	T	6–3	249	Indiana
Starr, Bart	QB	6–1	197	Alabama
Taylor, Jim	FB	6–0	214	LSU
Thurston, Fuzzy	G	6–1	247	Valparaiso
Voss, Lloyd	T	6–4	256	Nebraska
Wood, Willie	DB	5–10	190	USC
Wright, Steve	T	6–6	250	Alabama

1966
14–2 (includes 35–10 Super Bowl I win over Kansas City)
Vince Lombardi, head coach

	Pos	Ht	Wt	College
Adderley, Herb	CB	6–0	205	Michigan State
Aldridge, Lionel	DE	6–3	254	Utah State
Anderson, Bill	TE	6–3	211	Tennessee
Anderson, Donny	RB	6–2	215	Texas Tech
Bowman, Ken	C	6–3	230	Wisconsin
Bratkowski, Zeke	QB	6–2	210	Georgia
Brown, Allen	TE	6–5	235	Mississippi
Brown, Bob	DE	6–5	260	Arkansas-Pine Bluff
Brown, Tom	DB	6–1	192	Maryland
Caffey, Lee Roy	LB	6–4	240	Texas A&M
Chandler, Don	K	6–2	215	Florida
Crutcher, Tommy	LB	6–4	230	TCU
Curry, Bill	C	6–3	235	Georgia Tech
Dale, Carroll	WR	6–2	200	Virginia Tech
Davis, Willie	DE	6–3	243	Grambling St.
Dowler, Boyd	WR	6–5	224	Colorado
Fleming, Marv	TE	6–4	232	Utah
Gillingham, Gale	G	6–3	255	Minnesota
Grabowski, Jim	RB	6–2	220	Illinois
Gregg, Forrest	T	6–4	249	SMU
Hart, Doug	DB	6–0	190	Texas-Arlington
Hathcock, Dave	DB	6–0	195	Memphis State
Hornung, Paul	HB	6–2	215	Notre Dame
Jeter, Bob	DB	6–1	200	Iowa
Jordan, Henry	DT	6–2	248	Virginia
Kostelnik, Ron	DT	6–4	260	Cincinnati
Kramer, Jerry	G	6–3	245	Idaho
Long, Bob	WR	6–3	205	Wichita State
Mack, Red	WR	5–10	180	Notre Dame
McGee, Max	E	6–3	205	Tulane
Nitschke, Ray	LB	6–3	235	Illinois
Pitts, Elijah	HB	6–1	210	Philander Smith
Robinson, Dave	LB	6–3	245	Penn State
Skoronski, Bob	T	6–3	249	Indiana
Starr, Bart	QB	6–1	197	Alabama
Taylor, Jim	FB	6–0	214	LSU
Thurston, Fuzzy	G	6–1	247	Valparaiso
Vandersea, Phil	LB	6–3	245	Massachusetts
Weatherwax, Jim	DT	6–7	260	Cal State-L.A.
Wood, Willie	DB	5–10	190	USC
Wright, Steve	T	6–6	250	Alabama

1967

12–4–1 (includes 33–14 Super Bowl II win over Oakland)
Vince Lombardi, head coach

	Pos	Ht	Wt	College
Adderley, Herb	CB	6–0	205	Michigan State
Aldridge, Lionel	DE	6–3	254	Utah State
Anderson, Donny	RB	6–2	215	Texas Tech
Bowman, Ken	C	6–3	230	Wisconsin
Bratkowski, Zeke	QB	6–2	210	Georgia
Brown, Allen	TE	6–5	235	Mississippi
Brown, Bob	DE	6–5	260	Arkansas-Pine Bluff
Brown, Tom	DB	6–1	192	Maryland
Caffey, Lee Roy	LB	6–4	240	Texas A&M
Capp, Dick	TE	6–4	240	Boston College
Chandler, Don	K	6–2	215	Florida
Crutcher, Tommy	LB	6–4	230	TCU
Dale, Carroll	WR	6–2	200	Virginia Tech
Davis, Willie	DE	6–3	243	Grambling St.
Dowler, Boyd	WR	6–5	224	Colorado
Flanigan, Jim	LB	6–3	240	Pittsburgh
Fleming, Marv	TE	6–4	232	Utah
Gillingham, Gale	G	6–3	255	Minnesota
Grabowski, Jim	RB	6–2	220	Illinois
Gregg, Forrest	T	6–4	249	SMU
Hart, Doug	DB	6–0	190	Texas-Arlington
Horn, Don	QB	6–2	195	San Diego State
Hyland, Bob	C-G	6–5	255	Boston College
James, Claudis	WR	6–2	190	Jackson State
Jeter, Bob	DB	6–1	200	Iowa
Jordan, Henry	DT	6–2	248	Virginia
Kostelnik, Ron	DT	6–4	260	Cincinnati
Kramer, Jerry	G	6–3	245	Idaho
Long, Bob	WR	6–3	205	Wichita State
McGee, Max	E	6–3	205	Tulane
Mercein, Chuck	RB	6–2	225	Yale
Nitschke, Ray	LB	6–3	235	Illinois
Pitts, Elijah	HB	6–1	210	Philander Smith
Robinson, Dave	LB	6–3	245	Penn State
Rowser, John	DB	6–1	190	Michigan
Skoronski, Bob	T	6–3	249	Indiana
Starr, Bart	QB	6–1	197	Alabama
Thurston, Fuzzy	G	6–1	247	Valparaiso
Weatherwax, Jim	DT	6–7	260	Cal State-L.A.
Williams, Travis	RB	6–1	210	Arizona State
Wilson, Ben	FB	6–0	225	USC
Wood, Willie	DB	5–10	190	USC
Wright, Steve	T	6–6	250	Alabama

1996

16–3 (includes 35–21 Super Bowl XXXI victory over New England)
Mike Holmgren, head coach

	Pos	Ht	Wt	College
Beebe, Don	WR	5–11	185	Chadron State
Bennett, Edgar	RB	6–0	217	Florida State
Bostic, James*	RB	5–11	225	Auburn
Brooks, Robert*	WR	6–0	180	South Carolina
Brown, Gary	T	6–4	315	Georgia Tech
Brown, Gilbert	DT	6–2	325	Kansas
Butler, LeRoy	S	6–0	200	Florida State
Carpenter, Rob*	WR	6–2	190	Syracuse
Chmura, Mark	TE	6–5	250	Boston College
Clavelle, Shannon	DT	6–2	287	Colorado
Cox, Ron	LB	6–2	235	Fresno State
Darkins, Chris*	RB	6–0	215	Minnesota
Dellenbach, Jeff	C	6–6	300	Wisconsin
Dorsett, Matthew*	CB	5–11	190	Southern
Dotson, Earl	T	6–3	315	Texas A&I
Dotson, Santana	DT	6–5	285	Baylor
Evans, Doug	CB	6–0	190	Louisiana Tech
Favre, Brett	QB	6–2	225	Southern Miss
Flanagan, Mike*	C	6–5	290	UCLA
Freeman, Antonio	WR	6–0	187	Virginia Tech
Harris, Bernardo	LB	6–2	243	North Carolina
Hayes, Chris	S	6–0	200	Washington State
Henderson, William	RB	6–2	248	North Carolina
Hentrich, Craig	P	6–3	200	Notre Dame
Holland, Darius	DT	6–5	310	Colorado
Hollinquest, Lamont	LB	6–3	243	USC
Howard, Desmond	WR	5–10	180	Michigan
Jacke, Chris	K	6–0	205	Texas-El Paso
Jackson, Keith	TE	6–2	258	Oklahoma

	Pos	Ht	Wt	College
Jervey, Travis	RB	5–11	225	Citadel
Jones, Calvin	RB	5–11	205	Nebraska
Jones, Sean	DE	6–7	282	Northeastern
Knapp, Lindsay	G	6–6	300	Notre Dame
Koonce, George*	LB	6–1	243	East Carolina
Kuberski, Bob	DT	6–5	295	Navy
Levens, Dorsey	RB	6–1	235	Georgia Tech
Mayes, Derrick	WR	6–1	200	Notre Dame
McKenzie, Keith	DE-LB	6–3	242	Ball State
McMahon, Jim	QB	6–1	195	Brigham Young
Michels, John	T	6–7	290	USC
Mickens, Terry	WR	6–1	198	Florida A&M
Mullen, Roderick	CB-S	6–1	204	Grambling
Newsome, Craig	CB	6–0	188	Arizona State
Pederson, Doug	QB	6–3	215	N.E. Louisiana
Prior, Mike	S	6–0	208	Illinois State
Rison, Andre	WR	6–1	188	Michigan State
Rivera, Marco	G	6–4	295	Penn State
Robinson, Eugene	S	6–0	195	Colgate
Robinson, Michael	CB	6–1	192	Hampton
Simmons, Wayne	LB	6–3	248	Clemson
Taylor, Aaron	G	6–4	305	Notre Dame
Thomason, Jeff	TE	6–4	250	Oregon
Timmerman, Adam	G	6–4	295	South Dakota St.
Wachholtz, Kyle	QB	6–4	235	USC
White, Reggie	DE	6–5	300	Tennessee
Wilkerson, Bruce	T	6–5	305	Tennessee
Wilkins, Gabe	DE	6–4	305	Gardner-Webb
Williams, Brian	LB	6–2	235	USC
Williams, Tyrone	CB	5–11	195	Nebraska
Winters, Frank	C-G	6–3	285	Western Illinois

* Ended Season on Injured Reserve

BIBLIOGRAPHY

Bengtson, Phil with Todd Hunt. *Packer Dynasty*. Garden City, NY: Doubleday & Company, Inc., 1969.

Cameron, Steve. *The Packers!* Dallas: Taylor Publishing, 1996.

Carroll, Bob and Gershman, Neft, Thorn, et al. *Total Football II: The Official Encyclopedia of the National Football League*. New York: HarperCollins, 1999.

Collins, Tom. *The Green Bay Packer Hall of Fame: The Tradition Lives On!* Green Bay, Wis.: Green Bay Packer Hall of Fame, 1995.

Davenport, Don. *Green Bay Packers: Titletown Trivia Teasers*. Madison Wis.: Prairie Oak Press, 1997.

Davis, Willie. Personal interview. 14 May 2003.

Edelstein, Daniel. *The Packer Fan(atic) Handbook*. Oregon, Wis.: Badger Books Inc., 1999.

Favre, Brett with Chris Havel. *Favre: For the Record*. New York: Doubleday, 1997.

Gentile, Domenic with Gary D'Amato. *The Packer Tapes: My 32 Years with the Green*

Bay Packers. Madison, Wis..: Prairie Oak Press, 1995.

Goska, Eric. *Packer Legends in Facts: The Green Bay Packers 1919–1995*. Germantown, Wis.: Tech/Data Publications, 1995.

Goska, Eric. *Green Bay Packers: A Measure of Greatness*. Iola, Wis.: Krause Publications, 2003.

Grange, Red. "1919 Packers Earned $1.45 in Each Game." *Chicago Tribune*. 19 August, 1937.

Grange, Red. "Grange Tells How Packers Rose to Title." *Chicago Tribune*. 21 August, 1937.

Gruver, Ed. *The Ice Bowl: The Cold Truth about Football's Most Unforgettable Game*. Ithaca, NY: McBooks Press, 1998.

Korth, Todd. *Greatest Moments in Green Bay Packers Football History*. Lenexa, Kan.: Addax Publishing Group, 1998.

Lea, Bud with Vernon Biever and John Biever. *Magnificent Seven: The Championship Games That Built the Lombardi Dynasty*. Chicago: Triumph Books, 2002.

Maraniss, David. *When Pride Still Mattered: A Life of Vince Lombardi*. New York: Simon & Schuster, 1999.

McGinn, Bob. *The Road to Glory: The Inside Story of the Packers' Super Bowl XXXI Championship Season*. Louisville: AdCraft Sports Marketing, 1997.

Mihoces, Gary. "No surgery for Favre." *USA Today*. 15 January, 2004: 8C.

Mishler, Todd. *Cold Wars: 40 Years of Packer-Viking Rivalry*. Black Earth, Wis.: Prairie Oak Press, 2002.

Names, Larry D. *The History of the Green Bay Packers, Book I: The Lambeau Years, Part One*. Wautoma, Wis.: Angel Press of Wisconsin, 1987.

Names, Larry D. *The History of the Green Bay Packers, Book II: The Lambeau Years, Part Two*. Wautoma, Wis.: Angel Press of Wisconsin, 1989.

Names, Larry. *The World Champion Green Bay Packers Facts & Trivia, 5th Edition*. South Bend, Ind.: E.B. Houchin Company, 1997.

Nitschke, Ray and Robert W. Wells. *Mean on Sunday*.

Madison, Wis..: Prairie Oak Press, 1999.

Noble, Brian. Personal interview. 20 February, 2004.

Poling, Jerry. *Downfield! Untold Stories of the Green Bay Packers*. Madison, Wis.: Prairie Oak Press, 1996.

Ross, Alan. "No Brain, No Gain." *Sporting News Special Collectors' Edition: Pro Football's Tough Guys*. 2003: 71.

Schaap, Dick. *Green Bay Replay: The Packers' Return to Glory*. New York: Avon Books, 1997.

Swain, Glenn. *Packers vs. Bears*. Los Angeles: Charles Publishing, 1996.

Torinus, John B. *The Packer Legend: An Inside Look at the Green Bay Packers*. Neshkoro, Wis.: Laranmark Press, 1985.

Wagner, Len. *Launching the Glory Years: The 1959 Packers*. Coach's Books, LLC, 2001.

Ward, Arch. *The Green Bay Packers: The Story of Professional Football*. New York: G.P. Putnam's Sons, 1946.

Weisman, Larry. "Packers run with Seahawks' lone mistake." *USA Today*. 5 January, 2004: 3C.

Weisman, Larry. "For toughness over time, Brett Favre is No. 1." *USA Today*. 20 February, 2004: 3C.

Wood, Skip. "Joy follows grief for victorious Favre, Pack." *USA Today*. 29 December 2003: 3C.

Wood, Skip. "Packers steal win in overtime; Colts romp." *USA Today*. 5 January, 2004: 1C.

Zimmerman, David. *In Search of a Hero: Life and Times of Tony Canadeo, Packers' Gray Ghost*. Hales Corners, Wis.: Eagle Books, 2001.

Zimmerman, Paul. *The Linebackers: The Tough Ones of Pro Football*. New York: Scholastic Book Services, 1973.

INDEX

A

Adderley, Herb, 128, 192, 206-207, 212, 256-260
Agajanian, Ben, 116, 256
Aldridge, Lionel, 76, 258-260
Allen, Larry, 201
American Football League, 179-180
  AFL Championship Game, 180
  AFL-NFL World Championship Game, 179
Anderson, Donny, 58, 184, 259-260
Andrie, George, 147
Arizona Cardinals, 242
Arness, James, 221
Ashmore, Roger, 250
Atlanta Falcons, 70, 130, 219

B

Baker, Frank, 252
Baker, Roy "Bullet," 250
Baltimore Colts, 66, 170, 172
Baugh, Sammy, 123, 133
Bear Week, 230
Beebe, Don, 74, 261
Bellevue Park, 216
Bengtson, Phil, 75, 206
Bennett, Edgar, 43, 261
Biolo, John, 254
Blaik, Red, 81, 123
Bloodgood, Elbert "Al," 251
Blount, Mel, 207
Boeke, Jim, 177
Bostic, James, 261
Boston Celtics, 249
Boston Redskins, 162, 253
Bowdoin, James, 251

Bowman, Ken, 60, 159, 183-184, 258-260
Bradshaw, Terry, 123
Bratkowski, Zeke, 65, 172, 181, 258-260
Brennan, Jack, 254
Brickhouse, Jack, 231
Brock, Charley "Ears," 254-255
Brock, Lou, 255
Brockington, John, 158, 214
Brooks, Robert, 21-22, 44, 71, 261
Brookshier, Tom, 152
Brown, Bob, 56-57, 259-260
Brown, Gary, 261
Brown, Gilbert, 30, 261
Brown, Jim, 76, 173, 200
Brown, Paul, 100
Brown, Tom, 151, 178, 258-260
Bruder, Hank, 252-254
Buchanon, Willie, 192, 208
Buck, Howard "Cub," 29
Buffalo Bills, 180
Buffone, Doug, 233-234
Buhler, Larry, 254
Butkus, Dick, 126, 204
Butler, Frank, 253
Butler, LeRoy, 73, 261

C

Caffey, Lee Roy, 258-260
Cain, Joe, 234
Cahoon, Ivan, 250
Calhoun, George Whitney, 46, 248
Cameron, Steve, 21
Canadeo, Ruth, 245

Canadeo, Tony, 69, 100, 108-112, 193, 214, 230, 245, 255
Capp, Dick, 260
Carlos, Don, 252
Carmichael, Al, 212
Carolina Panthers, 188
Carpenter, Lew, 256-257
Carpenter, Rob, 261
Carter, Cris, 225, 237
CBS-TV, 147, 152, 155, 179
Chandler, Don, 76, 151, 170-171, 209, 258-260
Chicago Bears, 16, 37, 95, 107, 126, 137-138, 141, 161, 165, 204-205, 227-236, 244
Chicago Tribune, 34
Chmura, Mark, 261
Christiansen, Jack, 203, 207
Cincinnati Bengals, 70, 185
City Stadium, 143, 165, 216-217, 220-221
Clark, Monte, 124
Clavelle, Shannon, 261
Clemens, Cal, 253
Cleveland Browns, 65-66, 76, 170, 172-174, 258
Cochran, John "Red," 85
Coffey, Junior, 258
Comp, Irv, 164, 255
Connor, George, 231-232
Cope, Myron, 99
Cosby, Bill, 72
Cotton Bowl, 177
County Stadium, 218-220
Cox, Ron, 261
Craig, Larry "Superman," 209, 254-255

Croft, Milburn "Tiny," 255
Crutcher, Tommy, 258-260
Currie, Dan, 256-257
Curry, Bill, 258-259

D
Dale, Carroll, 175, 258-260
Dallas Cowboys, 45, 147, 149,
  151, 153, 176-178, 201, 225,
  239
Darling, Bernard "Boob," 250
Davenport, Don, 14, 16, 139,
  163, 216, 218, 220, 230, 252
Davenport, Wayne "Mike," 252
Davidson, Ben, 256
Davis, Willie, 19, 24, 27-28, 39,
  60-61, 97, 124-126, 128, 149,
  192, 203, 256-260
Dellenbach, Jeff, 261
Denver Broncos, 134
Detroit Lions, 36, 38, 143, 203
Dickey, Lynn, 53
Dillon, Bobby, 37-38, 192, 207-208
Dilweg, LaVern "Lavvie," 33, 35,
  105, 250-252
Dishman, Cris, 190, 236
Ditka, Mike, 124, 206, 236
Dorsett, Matthew, 261
Dotson, Earl, 261
Dotson, Santana, 30, 261
Dowler, Boyd, 32, 214, 256-260
Driver, Donald, 52
Duhart, Paul, 255
Dunn, Joseph "Red," 34, 250-252

E
Earp, Francis "Jug," 29, 35, 250-
  252
Ebert, John, 84
Edelstein, Daniel, 18, 68, 150
Eisenreich, Ted, 27
Elway, John, 134, 186
Engebretsen, Paul "Tiny," 253-
  254

Engelmann, Wuert, 251-252
ESPN, 78
Evans, Doug, 261
Evans, Jack, 250
Evans, Lon, 253
Evans, Vince, 244

F
Facenda, John, 98
Favre, Brett, 8, 15, 19, 21-22,
  24, 26-28, 30, 42-44, 48-50,
  54, 56, 59, 66, 70-73, 113,
  116, 123, 128, 130-134, 185,
  188-191, 201, 214-215, 239,
  241-244, 247, 261
Favre, Irvin, 48
Favre, Jeff, 48
Favre, Scott, 48
Feathers, Beattie, 137
First United Church of Christ,
  248
Fitzgibbon, Paul, 251-252
Flanagan, Mike, 261
Flanigan, Jim, 235, 260
Fleming, Marv, 258-260
Flowers, Bob, 255
Folkins, Lee, 256
Ford, Jim, 141
Forester, Bill, 256-257
Forte, Bob, 243
Foxx, Redd, 72
Franta, Herb "Chief," 251
Freeman, Antonio, 44, 190, 236-
  237, 261
Fritsch, Ted, 164, 255

G
Gassert, Ron, 257
Gentile, Domenic, 53-57, 59-60,
  119, 121, 123, 131, 175, 204
Gifford, Frank, 114, 147, 155
Gillespie, Earl, 111
Gillingham, Gale, 194, 259-260
Glanville, Jerry, 70

Goldenberg, Charles "Buckets,"
  253-255
Gordon, Lou, 253
Goska, Eric, 244, 247-248
Grabowski, Jim, 176, 259-260
Graham, Otto, 123
Grange, Red, 16, 33, 35, 103,
  194
Green, Ahman, 237
Green, Dennis, 236
Green Bay Press-Gazette, 160,
  248
Greenfield, Tom, 254
Gregg, Forrest, 60, 125, 128,
  192, 196, 236, 256-260
Gremminger, Hank, 256-258
Grimm, Dan, 258
Gros, Earl, 257

H
Hackbart, Dale, 224
Hagemeister Park, 160, 216
Halas, George, 95, 141-142, 228
Hallman, Curley, 131
Hallstrom, Ron, 70
Hampton, Dave, 212
Hanner, Dave "Hawg," 192, 202,
  256-257
Harlan, Bob, 186, 226
Harris, Al, 240
Harris, Bernardo, 261
Hart, Doug, 258-260
Hasselbeck, Matt, 240
Havel, Chris, 49
Havel, Ron, 130
Haycraft, Ken, 251
Hayes, Bob, 151
Hayes, Chris, 261
Henderson, William, 261
Hentrich, Craig, 209, 261-262
Herber, Arnie, 31, 35, 104, 137-
  138, 162, 251-254
Hill, Don, 250
Hill, Harlon, 37, 232

Hogan, Ben, 79

Holmgren, Mike, 22, 42, 50, 74, 113, 197, 261

Hornung, Paul, 22, 74, 77, 114-116, 152, 167, 181, 192, 200, 214, 247, 256-259

Houston Oilers, 70

Howard, Desmond, 44, 187, 192, 211, 261

Howton, Billy, 32, 165

Hubbard, Calvin "Cal," 35, 67, 78, 101, 105, 192, 194, 213, 250-252

Huff, Sam, 61, 63, 126

Hutson, Don, 31-32, 69, 78, 99, 135-139, *140*, 141-144, 162, 164, 192-193, 210, 214, 253-255

Hyland, Bob, 260

I

Ice Bowl, 51, 58, 145-155, 157, 159, 182, 184, 225

Iman, Ken, 256-257

Indian Packing Company, 14

Isbell, Cecil, 31, 35, 142, 163, 248, 254

J

Jacke, Chris, 261

Jackson, Keith, 261

Jacobs, Allen, 258

Jacunski, Harry, 254-255

James, Claudis, 260

Jankowski, Ed, 254

Jenison, Ray, 252

Jervey, Travis, 262

Jeter, Bob, 258-260

Johnson, Lyndon, 19

Johnston, Chester "Swede," 252-253

Jones, Sean, 19, 74, 262

Jordan, Henry, 68, 94, 116-117, 192, 202, 256-260

Jordan, Michael, 136

Jurgensen, Sonny, 97

K

Kahler, Bob, 255

Kansas City Chiefs, 179-180, 259

Kell, Paul, 254

Kercher, Bob, 255

Kern, William, 250-251

Kiesling, Walt "Babe," 253

Kilbourne, Wally "Cleats," 254

Knafelc, Gary, 148, 231, 256-257

Knapp, Lindsay, 262

Koonce, George, 262

Kostelnik, Ron, 256-260

Kotal, Eddie, 250

Kramer, Jerry, 20, 11, 39-41, 93, 98, 128, 170, 183-184, 192, 196, 198, 238, 256-260

Kramer, Ron, 256-257

Kuberski, Bob, 262

Kukar, Bernie, 240

Kuusisto, Bill, 255

L

Lambeau, Earl "Curly," 8, 14-15, 23-24, 35, 46, 78, 100, 136, 161, 213, 220, 243, 245, 250-255

Lambeau Field, 8, 27, 52, 58, 66, 70, 80, 145, 148-150, 154, 165, 184, 187, 215, 220, 222-223, 225, 227

Lambeau Leap, 21-22, 71

Landry, Tom, 45

Lane, Chuck, 96

Lane, Dick "Night Train," 207

Larson, Greg, 166

Lawrence, Jimmy, 254

Laws, Joe, 253-255

Lea, Bud, 61, 145-147, 154, 156-157, 165-166, 169, 171, 174, 176, 178-180, 184

Lee, Bill, 254

Lee, Carl, 224

Letlow, Russ, 253-254

Levens, Dorsey, 262

Lewellen, Verne, 30-31, 250-252

Lidberg, Carl "Cully," 250-251

Lilly, Bob, 147

Lofton, James, 32

Lombardi, Marie, 93

Lombardi, Vince, 1-2, 4-5, 8, 20-22, 24, 27-28, 39, 41-42, 45, 47-48, 51, 58, 60, 66, 68-69, 72-73, 75, 79-98, 100, 114, 116-121, 123-125, 150, 152, 156, 166-168, 177, 180, 182, 184, 191-192, 195-196, 200, 202-204, 206, 213, 225, 256-260

Longwell, Ryan, 192, 210

Los Angeles Rams, 20, 73

Los Angeles Times, 79

Luckman, Sid, 123

Lumberjack Band, 18

M

Madden, John, 133, 215

Maraniss, David, 15, 20, 24, 31, 81-82, 93-94, 125, 148, 154-155, 184

Marino, Dan, 123

Marshall, Bud, 258

Marshall, George, 162

Martinkovic, John, 217

Mason, Joel, 255

Masters, Norm, 256-257

Mattos, Harry, 253

Mayes, Derrick, 262

McCrary, Herdis, 250-252

McGee, Max, 32, 75, 77, 177, 181, 192, 209, 256-260

McGinn, Bob, 211

McKay, Roy "Tex," 255

McKenzie, Keith, 262

McMahon, Jim, 74, 134, 262

McNally, Johnny "Blood, 25," 31-32, 47, 78, 99, 101-103, 105, 191-192, 199, 213, 250-253

McPherson, Forrest, 255

Mercein, Chuck, 149-150, 182-184, 260

Meredith, Don, 178

Metropolitan Stadium, 158, 238

Miami Dolphins, 225

Michaels, Lou, 170

Michalske, August "Mike," 18, 35, 101, 105, 192, 194, 213, 250-252

Michels, John, 262

Mickens, Terry, 262

Miller, Paul, 253

Milwaukee Braves, 218

Milwaukee Brewers, 218

Minick, Paul, 250

Minneapolis Marines, 160

Minnesota Vikings, 56, 185, 190, 242

Mishler, Todd, 218-219, 222-223

Monday Night Football, 133, 235-236, 242

Montana, Joe, 42, 123

Montreal Canadiens, 249

Moore, Al, 254

Moore, Tom, 116, 256-258

Mullen, Roderick, 262

Mulleneaux, Carl "Moose," 254

Murray, Jim, 79

N

Nagurski, Bronko, 106-107, 138, 205

Namath, Joe, 59, 123

Names, Larry, 18, 31-32, 34-36, 101, 104-106, 128, 136, 141-144, 199, 216, 221-222, 226, 228-229

National Basketball Association, 136, 249

National Football Conference

NFC Central Division, 158, 185

NFC Championship Game, 188, 239

NFC Divisional Playoff, 187, 211

NFC Western Conference Playoff, 170-172, 219

NFC Wild Card Game, 52

National Football League, 7-9, 11, 25, 28, 32, 46, 64, 101, 103, 105, 119, 123, 135-137, 139, 141-142, 144, 147, 156, 160-161, 169-170, 176, 179-180, 191, 193-194, 198, 200-201, 205, 208, 212-214, 219, 222-223, 227, 229, 239, 246-247, 249

NFL Championship Game, 9, 11, 28, 36, 58, 61, 63, 66, 76, 145, 157, 159, 163-168, 170, 172-175, 177-178, 182-184, 204, 253-258

NFL Films, 98

Neely, Ralph, 153

Nelson, Darrin, 223

New City Stadium, 165, 220-221

New England Patriots, 189, 261

New York Giants, 9-11, 28, 42, 47, 61, 63-64, 139, 142, 156, 160, 163-169, 218, 256-257

New York Jets, 59

New York Yankees, 9, 249

Newsome, Craig, 262

Nitschke, Ray, 19, 28, 71, 118, 126-127, 155, 173, 192, 204, 207, 214, 233, 256-260

Nixon, Richard M., 221

Noble, Brian, 246

O

Oakland Raiders, 133, 242, 260

O'Bradovich, Ed, 126

Odom, Steve, 212

O'Donnell, Dick, 250-251

P

Packer Hall of Fame, 55, 143

Packers Foundation, 244

Pape, Oren "Nanny," 251

Parilli, Babe, 165

Paulekas, Tony, 253

Pederson, Doug, 262

Perkins, Don "Butch," 255

Perry, Claude "Cupid," 250-252

Philadelphia Eagles, 52, 97, 195

Pietrosante, Nick, 214

Pitts, Elijah, 256-260

Poling, Jerry, 38, 108-109, 112-113

Polo Grounds, 47, 160, 162

Primeau, Larry "the Packelope," 236-237

Pro Bowl, 37, 193, 195

Pro Football Hall of Fame, 39, 41, 78, 94, 143, 194, 222

Q

Quinlan, Bill, 256-257

R

Radick, Ken, 251-252

Reid, Floyd "Breezy," 247

Remmel, Lee, 20

Renfro, Mel, 176

Rice, Jerry, 44, 197

Ringo, Jim, 192, 195, 256-257

Rison, Andre, 262

Rivera, Marco, 262

Roach, John, 256-257

Robinson, Dave, 39, 66, 178, 185, 192, 203, 238, 258-260

Robinson, Michael, 262

Robustelli, Andy, 168

Rockne, Knute, 14

Ronzani, Gene, 36, 38, 243

Rose, Al "Big Un," 253

Rote, Tobin, 36

Ruth, Babe, 136

S

San Francisco 49ers, 27-28, 118, 186-187, 197, 203, 253-254

Sanders, Barry, 214

Sauer, George, 253
Saunders, Russ "Racehorse," 252
Schaap, Dick, 74, 77-78
Scherer, Bernie, 253
Schliebaum, Bill, 154
Schneidman, Herm, 253-254
Schultz, Charlie, 254
Schwammel, Ade, 253, 255
Scott, Ray, 51
Seattle Seahawks, 52, 240
Seven Blocks of Granite, 81
Sharpe, Sterling, 32, 54, 192, 197
Sherman, Mike, 241
Simmons, Wayne, 262
Skoronski, Bob, 173, 256-260
Sleight, Elmer "Red," 251-252
Smith, Ernie, 138, 253-254
Smith, Richard "Red," 250
Sorenson, Glen "Goof," 255
Soldier Field, 234-235
Sports Illustrated, 223
Sports Reporters, The, 78
Stahlman, Dick, 252
Starr, Bart, 19, 42, 51, 55, 58,
  65, 72-73, 75, 88, 95-96, 119-
  124, 146, 149, 155, 159, 169,
  171-172, 175, 182, 191-192,
  198, 214, 256-260
Starret, Ben, 255
State Fair Park, 139, 163, 218-
  219
Staten Island Stapletons, 17, 67
Staubach, Roger, 71
Steen, Frank, 254
Stram, Hank, 180
Sullivan-Wallen American Legion
  Post, 244
Super Bowl I, 77, 179-181, 209,
  259
Super Bowl II, 260
Super Bowl XXXI, 19, 26, 74, 77,
  189, 211, 248, 261
Svendsen, George, 253-254

Swain, Glenn, 228-229
Switzer, Veryl, 231-232

T

Tagliabue, Paul, 227
Tarkenton, Fran, 123, 185
Tassos, Damon, 109
Taylor, Kitrick, 185
Texas Stadium, 239
Thomason, Bob, 36
Thomason, Jeff, 262
Thompson Stadium, 17
Thompson, Tommy, 211
Thompson, Tuffy, 254
Thurston, Fuzzy, 20, 39, 41, 49,
  92, 256-260
Timmerman, Adam, 262
Tinsley, Pete, 254-255
Titletown Brewery, 78
Tittle, Y. A., 169, 214
Toburen, Nelson, 256-257
Tollefson, Chuck, 255
Torinus, John B., 14, 17, 29-30,
  33, 36-37, 46, 100-101, 104,
  107, 135, 138-139, 141, 143-
  144, 160, 162, 216-217
Tunnell, Emlen, 42, 207, 256
Turner, Clyde "Bulldog," 107
Twedell, Frank, 254

U

Unitas, Johnny, 123
Uram, Andy, 254
USA Today, 66

V

Van Derbur, Marilyn, 221
Voigt, Stu, 238
Voss, Lloyd, 258

W

Wachholtz, Kyle, 262
Ward, Arch, 34, 67, 102-103,
  164, 228
Warmath, Murray, 123
Washington Redskins, 97
WBAY-TV, 69
Weatherwax, Jim, 259-260
Wehba, Ray, 255
Weisgerber, Dick, 254
Weisman, Larry, 66
West, Ed, 220
WGN, 231
White, Reggie, 28, 72, 128-129,
  186, 192, 201, 248, 262
Whittenton, Jesse, 256-257
Wildung, Dick, 243
Wilkerson, Bruce, 262
Wilkins, Gabe, 262
Williams, Brian, 262
Williams, Clarence, 185
Williams, Howie, 257
Williams, Travis, 192, 212, 260
Williams, Tyrone, 262
Wilson, Ben, 260
Wilson, Faye "Mule," 260
Winters, Frank, 43, 262
Woessner, Bob, 151
Wolf, Ron, 13, 44, 130
Wood, Willie, 19, 124, 146, 192,
  206-207, 256-260
Woodin, Howard "Whitey," 250-
  252
Wright, Steve, 258-260
Wrigley Field, 138, 231, 233

Y

Yankee Stadium, 9-10, 61, 156-
  157, 168-169

Z

Zarnas, Gust, 254
Zimmerman, David, 108
Zoll, Dick, 254
Zuidmulder, Dave, 250-252
Zuver, Merle, 251